You'll Lose
the Baby Weight

You'll Lose
the Baby Weight

·······································

(And Other Lies about
Pregnancy and Childbirth)

·······································

DAWN MEEHAN

HOWARD BOOKS
A DIVISION OF SIMON & SCHUSTER, INC.

New York   Nashville   London   Toronto   Sydney

Howard Books
A Division of Simon & Schuster, Inc.
1230 Avenue of the Americas
New York, NY 10020

First Howard Books trade paperback edition November 2010

HOWARD and colophon are trademarks of Simon & Schuster, Inc.

For information about special discounts for bulk purchases, please contact Simon & Schuster Special Sales at 1-866-506-1949 or business@simonandschuster.com.

The Simon & Schuster Speakers Bureau can bring authors to your live event. For more information or to book an event, contact the Simon & Schuster Speakers Bureau at 1-866-248-3049 or visit our website at www.simonspeakers.com.

Designed by Jaime Putorti

Manufactured in the United States of America

10 9 8 7 6 5 4 3 2 1

Library of Congress Cataloging-in-Publication Data

Meehan, Dawn.
  You'll lose the baby weight : and other lies about pregnancy and childbirth / Dawn Meehan.
      p. cm.
  1. Pregnancy—Popular works. 2. Childbirth—Popular works. I. Title.
    RG551.M437 2010
    618.2—dc22   2010008601

ISBN 978-1-4391-8380-9
ISBN 978-1-4391-9003-6 (ebook)

This book is dedicated to
Austin, Savannah, Jackson,
Lexington, Clayton, and Brooklyn,
my six little miracles and the joys of my life.

CONTENTS

CONTENTS

CONTENTS

You'll Lose
the Baby Weight

Best Things About Being Pregnant

. . . .

1. Feeling the baby move

2. Big boobs

3. Eating for two (or three or twelve)

4. No period for nine months!

5. You get a baby when it's all said and done!

Yeah, that's pretty much all I can think of.

CHAPTER 1

I'M NOT A DOCTOR;
I JUST PLAY ONE ON TV

When my husband and I got married, we discussed having children and came up with the plan to have two. That's when God laughed at us and came up with His own plan. Now, six kids (and 38,972 diapers) later, we are done. It's good that things didn't go according to our plans because one or two kids wouldn't have made my life chaotic enough to write about. Going through two pregnancies just wouldn't have made me miserable enough to feel the need to share all the hideous details with you. I think I needed to throw up at least 568,229 times in order to accurately describe morning sickness. I wouldn't have had enough experience with only two children, so it's all good.

From the time Eve gave birth to Cain and, later, his brother Abel, the miracle of childbirth has gone on. And it is indeed a miracle. When you take into consideration everything that has to happen in order to conceive and bear a baby, it's amazing that any babies are ever born. Only God could design a woman's body to be so perfectly suited to bearing and nurturing children. Those wide hips that we complain about, we suddenly find just right for housing a baby for nine months. The hormones responsible for the PMS we experience every month are exactly what we need to support a pregnancy. The breasts that won't fit into a comfortable bra now have a new purpose in feeding our babies.

Although I didn't always enjoy being pregnant at the time, I have to admit that every time I see a pregnant woman, I kind of miss it. Maybe it's because I know that the end result is worth any discomforts. Or more likely it's because when I'm pregnant, I have an excuse to eat for two and carry around a few extra pounds. When you first hold your precious little miracle, the little soul that God has entrusted to your care, all the aches and pains of pregnancy completely dissolve. Newborn babies come equipped with this addictive sweet smell, and one sniff of their warm little heads will have you hooked. This, coupled with pregnancy amnesia—a condition that causes you to forget all about the morning sickness, backaches, heartburn, and varicose veins—is the reason people have more than one baby.

Whether you're pregnant with your first or fifth baby or you're just thinking about being pregnant, let me just say right up front: "I'm not an actual doctor; I just play one on TV." This book is chock-full of fun stories about pregnancy and childbirth, but does not contain one bit of medical advice. It isn't intended as a medical guide, but more like my opinion of pregnancy-related *stuff*. In some cases, it's a "what not to do" guide, where I share my hard-learned les-

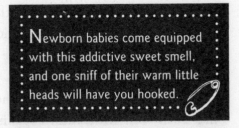

Newborn babies come equipped with this addictive sweet smell, and one sniff of their warm little heads will have you hooked.

sons of things that you might want to avoid (for example, gaining sixty-five pounds with your pregnancy). I'm not an obstetrician or a nurse or a midwife. I didn't go to medical school, and I have no real obstetrical knowledge. Then why am I writing this book? Because I have been pregnant and given birth six times. That means I've spent approximately fifty-four months, almost five years, of my life pregnant. I may not have actual medical training, but I sure do have a wealth of experience. And I'm here to share my stories with you because that's what women who have given birth do—they share their stories to ~~scare~~ enlighten others.

Although I can describe, with amazing accuracy, how badly you'll have to pee during an ultrasound, I can't tell you all the things a technician will look for during an ultrasound exam. I want this book to make you laugh until you wet your pants (because that's what pregnant women do). Then I want you to go to your doctor and ask him all your important questions. Understand? Come here to find out why you shouldn't name your new baby Schenectady; go to your doctor to find out why you're spotting. Come here to find out the best way to pee in a cup when you can't even see the cup around your big belly; go to your doctor to find out what the results of your urinalysis mean.

Seriously, please check in with your doctor or nurse-midwife with any questions you have. Pregnancy, especially first pregnancies, can be a little scary if you're unsure of what's going on with you and your baby. An actual MD (and not someone who just has the initials *M* and *D* in their name) can explain things to you and put your fears to rest. And while you're sitting in the waiting room, waiting to be seen by your doctor, read this book for a laugh or two.

I joke that the reason I have six kids is because I didn't want seven, but really, it's because I just love babies. I love the whole childbirth experience and I love, love, love that newborn baby smell and the sweet little sounds they make. In fact, writing this chapter is making me want "just one more." I'd better move on to some of the more unpleasant symptoms of pregnancy before I get too carried away . . .

Signs You're Ready to Start a Family

1. You've started shopping for a minivan.

2. You have so much money that you don't know what to do with it.

3. You want an excuse to go to Disney World.

4. You recently replaced your white carpeting with industrial-strength floor tile.

5. You love the smell of baby lotion.

6. You're tired of refilling your birth control pills every month.

7. Your biological clock is ticking.

8. You've already got your unborn child's name on a waiting list at the best preschool in town.

9. You're thinking that you're much too thin and need to gain a little weight.

10. You've trained yourself to get by on two and a half hours of sleep a night.

CHAPTER 2

SO, YOU WANT TO
START A FAMILY

Y ou're ready to start a family, you say. You and your husband have discussed having children (and hopefully agree about it). My husband and I had a hard time agreeing on when to start our family. I wanted to have babies right away. He wanted to wait until we were better off financially. We both felt strongly about our opinions and had a difficult time seeing the other's point of view. I finally convinced him it was like taking off a Band-Aid. You just have to rip it off! Just go for it! Eighteen years have passed since we had this discussion, and I'm happy to say that I was right and he was wrong! Seriously, if we'd waited until we were better off financially, we'd still be waiting. (And I just like saying that I was right and he was wrong.)

So you and your spouse have come to the conclusion that your lives are much too quiet. Your house is far

•9•

too clean, your furniture lacks scratches, your walls don't have any marker drawings, and your cars don't have twenty pounds of garbage scattered on the floor. You don't have any appliances held together with duct tape; you have way too much money, free time, and peace and quiet; so you feel the need to fill your days with poopy diapers, toys scattered all over your floor, and endless calls of "Mom!" "Mooom!" "MOOOOOM!"

Now what? What happens when the dream of having a baby becomes a reality? You're about to join the league of women who have given birth before you.

Am I Pregnant or Is Aunt Flo Knocking?

How can you tell if you're pregnant? First, you can wait. If you're pregnant, you'll eventually go into labor and then you'll know you're pregnant. Of course, most women figure out they're pregnant long before they go into labor. Unless you're that one woman a year who claims she didn't realize she was pregnant until, thinking she had indigestion, she went to the hospital in labor. I'll let you in on a secret. That one woman a year is lying. There is no way, I repeat—NO WAY—you could possibly not know you're pregnant for nine months. None. No way. If you've had a child, I know you're nodding your head in agreement with me right now. If you

> There is no way, I repeat—NO WAY—you could possibly not know you're pregnant for nine months.

haven't been pregnant yet, just read this book and you'll see what I mean. No. Way.

And even if you could, most women aren't willing to wait until they go into labor to find out if they're pregnant, and it wouldn't really be a wise thing to do anyway. I mean, you'd miss out on all the sympathy from friends, family, and complete strangers as you complain about your pregnancy aches and pains. And if you didn't know you were pregnant until you went into labor, no one would throw you a baby shower and you wouldn't get to gush over tiny, cute baby socks and tiny, cute diapers and tiny, cute overalls and, well, basically everything that's tiny and cute.

When you're first trying to figure out if you're pregnant, you look for signs that might indicate you're "in a family way." For example, I discovered I was pregnant with several of my babies when I walked into the grocery store and the mingling scents of fresh produce, salmon, roasted chicken, and birthday cake made me turn green and run for the exit before I gave the other shoppers a visual demonstration of morning sickness. On the bright side, it saved me from running out to buy a pregnancy test, which is a good thing because those babies are expensive! To this day, if I smell something funky that turns my stomach, I tend to freak out that I might be pregnant even when I'm sure that's not possible.

When we want a baby so badly, our minds can have a funny way of tricking our bodies into feeling pregnant even when they aren't. I tried to get pregnant for a year before I conceived my first baby. I remember thinking, month after month, that I was pregnant. I just *had* to be pregnant. I was

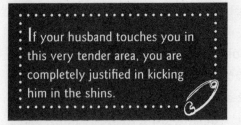

If your husband touches you in this very tender area, you are completely justified in kicking him in the shins.

certain I was feeling pregnancy symptoms because I wanted to be pregnant so badly. Conversely, if we don't feel quite ready to accept the responsibility of a new baby, we can sometimes trick ourselves into believing we're not actually pregnant when we are. I'm pretty sure I'd be in complete denial if I felt pregnancy symptoms today. In fact, I might even be one of those people who insisted she couldn't possibly be pregnant until the baby's head was crowning and I could no longer deny it. Still, there are some common signs and symptoms that can help you figure out whether you're pregnant or not.

BREAST TENDERNESS: Oftentimes, women who are newly pregnant experience pain and tenderness in their breasts. This starts approximately two seconds after you conceive. It's one of the earliest symptoms my friends and I experienced during our pregnancies. The tenderness and soreness can be quite intense, too. What this means is that wearing a bra can really hurt. Of course, not wearing a bra can really hurt, too. You won't be able to sleep on your stomach unless you want to feel like someone is hitting you in the chest with a baseball bat. If your husband touches you in this very tender area, you are completely justified in kicking him in the shins. It's not all bad, though, as this is the perfect excuse to stop jogging on that treadmill and to start using it as something more functional—like a clothes hanger. So if your breasts are tender and sore, you just might be pregnant.

MORNING SICKNESS: Another sign of possible pregnancy is the dreaded morning sickness. Although morning sickness doesn't usually start up in earnest until you're four to six weeks pregnant, if you're lucky, you could start feeling nauseous earlier than that. If you're lucky enough to have a toddler in diapers and you vomit repeatedly while changing smelly diapers, you just might be pregnant. This wasn't a problem when I was pregnant with my first baby, but I had at least one child in diapers with each subsequent pregnancy. It was not fun. A heightened sense of smell for both nasty and sweet scents is common in pregnancy, so if you suddenly find yourself smelling chocolate chip cookies from the bakery that's fifty-eight miles away, you could possibly be pregnant.

Of course, not all women experience morning sickness, so you may not ever have this symptom. If that's true for you, congratulations—I no longer like you. Go sit in the corner with my sister and sister-in-law, who never so much as hiccupped, let alone vomited, during their pregnancies.

MISSED PERIOD: A big sign of pregnancy is skipping your period for over a month. This is a pretty good indication of pregnancy, although stress can do funny things to your body, and what causes more stress than wondering if you're pregnant or not? This isn't a telltale sign if you're irregular to begin with. If you could set your clock by the monthly visit of dear Aunt Flo,

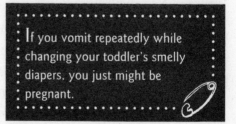

If you vomit repeatedly while changing your toddler's smelly diapers, you just might be pregnant.

then this sign is probably more reliable for you. This is one of the most pleasant symptoms of pregnancy. In fact, it may just be the best part of pregnancy, save giving birth to your new little baby. I mean, you get to go a whole nine months with no period! Kind of makes you want to get pregnant just for that little fringe benefit, doesn't it? But, as with all good things, this too must end, and after giving birth, let me tell ya, your uterus more than makes up for lost time.

FATIGUE: Being exhausted is another very common sign of pregnancy. During the first few months of pregnancy, I couldn't stay awake past 8:00 p.m., and I found myself nodding off while sitting at red lights during the day. If you fall asleep on your desk at work or in your chicken salad at lunch, there's a good chance you could be pregnant. I remember driving home on my lunch hour while I was pregnant with my first child. I'd get home and head toward the kitchen to make lunch, but I would pass out on the couch before I ever pulled out a plate. I *needed* those little naps. You may think you've experienced tiredness, but until you've gotten pregnant, you have no idea how that extreme pregnancy-fatigue feels. Even toothpicks in your eyelids can't keep your eyes open when you're newly pregnant. When I was pregnant with my first baby, I was certain I had mono. No way could pregnancy cause a person to be so tired. Clearly, there was something very wrong with me, I decided.

Of course, this sign isn't as noticeable in mothers who already have one or more children, since sleep deprivation and fatigue are pretty much a way of life for us moms.

MOOD SWINGS: And let's not forget the mood swings. Mood swings are very commonplace in pregnancy. My husband could usually tell I was pregnant when he said something innocuous like, "You look nice today," and instead of thanking him, I whipped my head around, shot laser beams from my eyes, and snapped, "What's *that* supposed to mean?!" While watching television, I'd see a commercial for car insurance and burst into tears. I just never knew what might set me off. I was a veritable Sybil throughout my pregnancies. And here's the thing about mood swings—you don't even realize you're nuts when you're pregnant. You can't clearly see your irrational behavior, and you'll most likely think that everyone else is irritable—not you.

Unfortunately, all the symptoms listed above are also signs that you're about to get your period. Nature is funny that way. Those sore breasts can mean that Dear Aunt Flo is knocking on your door. And food cravings . . . well who *doesn't* want chocolate once a month? I don't know about anyone else, but I personally have food cravings 360 days a year. (The other five days I have the flu.) I know for a fact that once a month, I become a sort of Mr. Hyde–like person who's liable to bite someone's head off for looking at me the wrong way (or so my friends insist). And sometimes your period

> I personally have food cravings 360 days a year. (The other five days I have the flu.)

is late because you're afraid your period might be late. Our bodies are just fun that way.

So how do you determine if your signs and symptoms are from pregnancy or impending menstruation? How can you tell if the nausea you feel is because there's a little person growing inside you or if it's because you just polished off a box of cookies? How do you know if you're slightly moody because in nine months, you'll have an addition to your family, or because your period is right around the corner, or because the kids just dumped an entire bottle of dishwashing soap on the kitchen floor so they could skate through it? It's a tough call and one that even seasoned mothers of multiple children have a hard time figuring out. But never fear. Thankfully there are a couple ways to answer the question, Am I pregnant?

It Only Takes Six (or More) Tests

The over-the-counter, store-bought pregnancy test can be very useful in determining whether you should be buying those skinny jeans you've had your eye on or whether you should opt instead for the *Big Book of Baby Names*. Home pregnancy tests have changed over the years and are now very easy to use. And they're so accurate that most women can get clear results as early as the first day of their missed period, sometimes even earlier.

Now, when you go to the store to purchase a pregnancy test, buy at least six of them. Seriously, you'll need that many unless you're like my friend Jane, who bought a pregnancy test and then, as a wave of morning sickness hit her, threw up on the way home from the store. She turned to her husband and said, "Looks like we just wasted ten dollars." The rest of us will need that many, and I'll tell you why. When you get home from the store, although the package directions say to use "first morning urine," you won't be able to wait until morning, so you'll open the package and test right away. After viewing the results, whether positive or negative, you won't believe their accuracy because you didn't perform the test first thing in the morning. Thus test number two. You take the second test first thing the next morning. After unwrapping the test stick, peeing on it, and waiting the requisite five minutes, you read the results. Is that a faint line you see? Could you be pregnant? As you start to get your hopes up, you realize that you neglected to lay the test on a flat surface. Oh no! The directions specifically say to lay the test stick down on a flat surface! You held the stick in your hand while watching for the line to darken. You can't count this test. It might not be accurate because it wasn't sitting flat for the five-minute wait.

You wonder if you can take another test right away. You're fresh out of first morning urine. Will it still count? You decide to open the package containing test number three and give it a shot. This time you make sure it's lying flat on the counter. Is that a line you see? It's so faint, you're not sure it's a line at all. So, now what? Are you not pregnant because you can't really see a line, or are you pregnant and the line is hardly visible simply because, once again, you didn't use first morning urine?

You opt to wait until the next morning to retest. But

later in the day, you decide you just can't wait that long, and you end up taking another one before you go to bed. Of course you can't rely on those results because, again, you didn't use first morning urine.

The next morning, you take one more test. It's positive, but since it's a generic, dollar-store test, you just don't believe the positive results, so you grab another name-brand test, but not wanting to waste yet another test, you manage to wait until the next morning to take it. So, you take the sixth test that next morning and with any luck, you get results that are clearly positive (or negative if that's what you're hoping for). We'll just concentrate on the positive here since this *is* a book on pregnancy. I have a couple friends who, even after getting a clearly positive result, would go out and buy a couple more tests "just to be sure." There's just something reassuring about seeing that little pink line, especially when you're newly pregnant and have no symptoms. This is your only confirmation that there's a new life growing inside you. Before you have visual confirmation from an ultrasound exam and before you feel the baby moving, you can pull out that pee stick and stare at those little pink lines to remind yourself that you are indeed pregnant. I have some friends who saved their positive pregnancy tests and put them in their children's baby books. That was a little too gross for me, though. I mean, I just PEED on it, for crying out loud. Although, truth be told, when I was cleaning out my desk the other day, I ran across a positive pregnancy test from about four years ago. (Yeah, I don't clean my desk very often apparently.) I have no idea why I even kept this thing (and in my desk, no less!), but there it was, and looking at it brought back those happy memories of first seeing that positive line.

> That little pink line is your only confirmation that there's a new life growing inside you.

Start Spreading the News

So you have the pee stick with the two pink lines. Now what? At some point you'll want to start spreading the good news to your husband, family, and friends. Some women (me) who don't have the patience to wait for a doctor's confirmation (me) might be tempted to start spreading the good news (me) right away. There's nothing wrong with that approach (and I'm not just saying this because it's what I did every single time). On the other hand, women with a modicum of patience might want to consider waiting until their physician confirms their suspicions, as those home pregnancy tests have been known to be wrong a time or two. I know many women who opt to wait until they're three months along before letting the cat out of the bag.

Either way, at some point you're going to want to share the news. Just how do you go about sharing the wonderful tidings with your significant other? How do you let the love of your life know that you'll soon be adding another member to your family? You'll want to make sure you announce this upcoming event in a special way. I mean, this will be a moment that you'll both remember forever. And of course you'll want to be able to write how the whole announcement unfolded in the baby book.

I had my own special creative ways of telling Joe that I was pregnant. When I was pregnant for the first time (and after trying for a year to get pregnant, I might add) I bought a card and a baby bottle. I made a special dinner and set the baby bottle by Joe's place at the dinner table. He came home from work, sat down to the table, saw the bottle, and said, "What's this?"

I answered him, beaming, excited, "It's a baby bottle!"

He replied, "Oh."

That's it.

Oh.

I burst into tears and wailed, "You don't love me! You don't even care!" Hey, I said pregnancy hormones can make otherwise-sane women act nuts.

After my fourth baby was born, I was happy and content. I had two girls and two boys, and they were all happy and healthy. Well, they were healthy anyway. My family seemed complete. Life was good. And then I got that pink line on the ole pregnancy test. A fifth baby? A FIFTH child??? Oh, I can't do this! I can't have any more! I started hyperventilating. I marched right out to the family room, where my husband had fallen asleep on the couch, and whipped the positive pee stick at him while demanding, "How the heck did THIS happen?!" This is probably not the best idea. This will not make for good, lasting memories. Wait, let me rephrase that. It will make for lasting memories, all right. It just won't make for *good* memories.

But never fear, God knew what He was doing when He blessed us with our fifth (and every other child, for that matter). Even though I thought I was done having kids, He had other plans. In fact, God blessed us with two more babies, and we couldn't have been happier about it.

When I realized I was pregnant with my sixth baby, I had the attitude of "What's one more?" I believe I got on the phone and informed my husband, "Remember when I told you to pack away the crib? Well, you don't have to do that after all. Five kids isn't really all that many, is it? Wouldn't six be more fun? You know, it's a nice, even number. The Bradys had six after all. Where did we put the atlas? I think we need another city name."

The choices for the announcement of your impending parenthood are plentiful. The sky's the limit. Here I've compiled a list of some creative, unique possibilities to help you make your announcement special. These are tried-and-true suggestions from real people who have used them.

SURPRISE YOUR HUSBAND BY FILLING PINK AND BLUE BALLOONS WITH HELIUM and letting them float up to the ceiling. When your husband enters the house and sees the ceiling covered with pink and blue, he'll think, *Wow! We're having a baby!* Either that, or he'll think you're trying to tell him that you're having twins. Or maybe that you're throwing a surprise party for him. Or perhaps that you're subtly trying to tell him that he's forgotten your anniversary. I'm pretty sure my husband wouldn't have picked up on the subtlety of

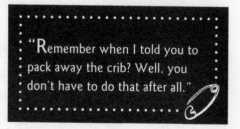

"Remember when I told you to pack away the crib? Well, you don't have to do that after all."

the balloons. That, and the fact that I hate the squeaky sound of balloons, made this an idea I was definitely not willing to try.

COOK YOUR HUBBY A SPECIAL DINNER OF BABY CORN, BABY BACK RIBS, AND BABY SPINACH. Set the table with a little pot of baby's breath for the centerpiece. Just keep in mind that men can be kinda slow and there's a good chance he won't catch on to your well-thought-out dinner theme. Be prepared to explain the significance of all the baby food. Unfortunately, having to explain why you made baby corn and baby back ribs to your husband who, in your opinion, should automatically know what you're doing, can kinda take the steam out of the announcement. And I've been told that BBQ sauce is really hard to get off the walls. What? I've never thrown BBQ ribs at my husband's head. I've just heard.

GIVE HIM A GIFT. You can give him a T-shirt that reads "World's Best Dad" or a picture frame with the words "Dad and Me" inscribed on it or a coffee mug that reads, "I Love Daddy." These are simple gifts that are easy to order and personalize, and most husbands will catch on to the message behind the gift. Unless, of course, he thinks you goofed up and meant to give it to your dad.

PAINT, "YOU'RE GOING TO BE A DAD" ON THE INSIDE BOTTOM OF A COFFEE MUG OR SOUP BOWL. Fill the mug with coffee or the bowl with soup or cereal or ice cream and watch for his reaction when he gets to the bottom and sees the message. You can use a paint pen to write your message or go to a paint-your-own-ceramics place to do it.

PUT TOGETHER A SLIDE SHOW OF PICTURES FOR HIM. If you're computer savvy, you can do this yourself on your computer and burn it to a DVD. Include pictures of you two as babies, pictures of you dating, pictures of your wedding, and then at the end add a picture of baby booties or a crib along with your due date. Many stores offer services like this (in many cases, you can do it yourself at the store with the help of an employee) for those who aren't so computer literate. Then make a bowl of popcorn, cuddle up on the couch with the unsuspecting dad, pop the DVD into the machine, and watch his reaction.

Things to Do Before Getting Weighed at Your Appointment

1. Dress in lightweight clothing.

2. Take off your shoes.

3. Take off your coat.

4. Take your keys out of your pocket.

5. Take your cell phone out of your pocket.

6. Trim your nails.

7. Blow your nose.

8. Tweeze your eyebrows.

9. Get a haircut.

10. Go to the bathroom.

CHAPTER 3

TESTING 1, 2, 3

Throughout your pregnancy, you'll have many tests. Even with the most low-risk pregnancies, there will be a myriad of tests. Most of these are routine and they're used simply to reassure the doctor and you that everything is going smoothly and developing as it should. Here, I'll give you a rundown of the more common tests you'll probably be given during your pregnancy. You may not have all of these, or you may have all these and then some. It really all depends on how good your insurance is and how many kids your doctor has to put through college.

At your first appointment you'll most likely have a battery of tests. They'll check your height and weight and blood pressure. They may do a pregnancy test to confirm your pregnancy. The obstetrician I used for my first four pregnancies never gave me a pregnancy test. She believed me when I told her I was pregnant. The obstetrician I used for my last two babies did a blood test to confirm my pregnancies. The fact that I'd already given birth four times and I *knew* I was pregnant didn't count. My doctors insisted I give them some blood so they could ~~charge me more money to pay for their kid's braces~~ make certain I was pregnant.

Your caregiver will probably do a complete physical and take down your medical history. They'll probably draw a couple, or thirty, vials of blood for tests. Finally, they're bound to do an internal exam and Pap smear at this first appointment. I know you're thinking what a drag it is to have a Pap smear. You hate having to undress and lie there on the table for that particular kind of exam. It's just so embarrassing having a virtual stranger get that up close and personal, right? I guess I should warn you that you'll have a whole team of medical personnel who are that up close and personal in the very near future, and you won't even think twice about it. Honestly! I know you probably don't believe me now, but when you're in labor and you have 532 people in your room, staring up your birth canal (and later when seventeen people are handling your boobs to help you nurse your baby), you won't care one little bit. Somehow, modesty goes out the window during labor and childbirth.

Let the ~~Embarrassment~~ Fun Begin!

You probably already know how Paps go, but I'll refresh your memory here so there aren't any surprises. You walk into the exam room and after the nurse has finished taking your blood pressure and such, she'll hand you a ~~piece of paper with armholes cut into it~~ gown and leave for you to change. When she leaves, you have to change as quickly as

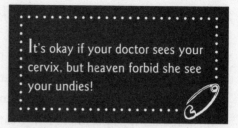

It's okay if your doctor sees your cervix, but heaven forbid she see your undies!

you possibly can to ensure you're completely covered by the time the doctor walks in. It doesn't matter that the doctor is going to have her hand shoved up to your cervix; she must not see you changing because that would just be embarrassing! After pulling off your clothes, neatly fold your underwear and carefully tuck it into your jeans. It's okay if your doctor sees your cervix, but heaven forbid she see your undies! I mean, who knows what your doctor would do with that sort of information! Maybe the doctors and nurses have a poll going to see which patients wear grandma-pants and which ones wear thongs. All I know is that I'm not going to take that kind of chance, so I've always carefully hidden my underwear away from prying eyes. Hmmm, now that I think about it, I'm wondering if my doctor thinks I don't wear underwear at all! Oh no! I'd never considered that possibility before. Oh great, I'm probably known in that office as the weirdo who goes commando.

Next, neatly stack your clothes on the chair and hop up onto the table, which is covered with a soft layer of paper for your comfort. You need to get on that table as quickly as you can so the doctor doesn't inadvertently walk in while your bare butt is hanging out of your paper-doll cover-up. If you usually have a long wait until your doctor makes an appearance, grab a magazine to read before settling yourself on the exam table. This is important and I'll tell you why.

One time, I waited and waited for my doctor to walk in. I was bored, so I thought I'd thumb through a magazine. The only problem was that the magazines were in a rack on the wall opposite of where I sat, on the table. I considered hopping down to grab the magazine, but I figured the moment I leapt from the table, the doctor would waltz in and see me walking around the room, gown agape, and we all know that unwritten rule that states you must be seated on the table when the doctor walks in with your paper blanket pulled neatly around you. I thought perhaps if I leaned over just a bit, I could reach the magazine from the table. I stretched my arm out and wiggled my fingers, trying to grasp the edge of the magazine rack. I leaned a little farther. I braced myself with one hand while extending my other arm as far as I possibly could. I could almost touch it. Just one more inch. Almost there. And then I fell. I landed in a heap on the floor just as the doctor walked in. It's hard to feel ~~like you're not a total loser~~ classy when you're sitting on the floor with your butt hanging out of a paper gown. And this, my friend, is why you want to grab the magazine *before* sitting on the table.

After the doctor makes small talk with you, she'll ask you to get in position. This means you lie on your back and scoot down until your butt hangs off the end of the table. Then you put your feet up in the air in devices called stirrups, but don't be fooled by the name. This is *nothing* like horseback riding. Your doctor will then take a tool out of the freezer where it is stored. This tool looks similar to what is used for changing the tire on your car. She'll put this cold metal jack where the sun don't shine, and then she'll crank it open wide. At this point, you should really try to concentrate on the picture of the palm tree or the puppy or the faded, old Ziggy cartoon taped on the ceiling above you. No, it won't really distract you from the fact that a virtual stranger is poking around *down there,* but you can pretend.

Your physician will then take a large Q-tip and swab your cervix for a sample of cells. I tend to joke around in uncomfortable situations, and it doesn't get much more uncomfortable than this. If you want to lighten the mood while your doctor is performing this exam, ask her stuff like, "I lost my car keys yesterday. Can you see if they're in there?" Or maybe, "Hey, could you shove that Q-tip up any farther? Are you trying to clean my ears with that thing?" Or, it's always fun to throw them off with crazy, obscure small talk like, "So, if you had a pet hippo, what would you name him?" or, "How many candy canes do you think you could fit in your mouth at once?" Hey, you gotta do what you gotta do to get through these awkward exams, right?

Then you'll sit there on the table wondering if you should change into your clothes while the doctor is standing there talking to you, or if you should continue to sit there in your stylish paper gown while making small talk with the doctor until she leaves.

If you have other children, you'll want to schedule your internal-exam appointments at a time when you can get a babysitter. Trust me on this. With every pregnancy, save my first, I brought my little kids to the doctor with me for most of my appointments. It wasn't my first choice, but it wasn't easy to get a babysitter, so I did what I had to do. However, I made a great effort to find a sitter for the appointments when I knew I'd be having an internal exam. It's just not fun fielding questions from an inquisitive three-year-old. "Mom, what's that doctor doing? Why are you naked? Why is he touching your butt? Mom, where's your underwear?"

Baby's First Picture

Chances are, at some point in your pregnancy, you'll have at least one ultrasound, a test that sadistic doctors use as a method of torture. I know what you're thinking. You're thinking that you had an ultrasound and it wasn't painful. It wasn't an invasive test. What's the big deal? The only reason you're thinking this is because you've forgotten what it's really like. I'm here to refresh your memory and to give a heads-up to all of you who have yet to experience your first obstetrical ultrasound. It's what I do. No need to thank me.

If your doctor orders an ultrasound at some point in your pregnancy, you will have to do a couple things to prepare for this test. First, you must drink thirty-two ounces of water. That's the same thing as forty-four gallons. Second, you must hold it. That's right, your doctor is telling your compressed, pregnant bladder to hold twenty times its weight in urine and keep it there. Take this well-intentioned warning from

> An ultrasound is a test that sadistic doctors use as a method of torture.

me: Whatever you do, do not sneeze. Or cough. Or laugh. Pretty much just sit there, legs crossed, while bouncing up and down and praying the technician comes into the waiting room and calls you in for the test really, really soon.

Maybe some of you will be lucky enough to have your ultrasound done in a nice, newly redecorated hospital or medical facility. You know what I'm talking about? The kind of hospital that's been decorated to look more like a hotel lobby. You sit in the waiting room, surrounded by plants, comfortable overstuffed chairs (that you can't fully enjoy because you're busy trying not to pee on those nice over-stuffed chairs), soft music playing in the background, and a lovely, peaceful, soothing water fountain. As the water bub-bles up and runs in rivulets down the rocks, finally splash-ing into a pool, your bladder is saying, "I hear water—whole fountains of water. That must mean it's time to go!" Only by the grace of God do your muscles hold in the urine. This is especially true for seasoned mothers who have given birth a time or two before. Pregnancy does something to your bladder control, in that you no longer have any. If you've had more than one baby already, chances are you'll need a change of clothing at this point.

When it's your turn to go back and actually have the ul-trasound, you'll have to hoist your big ole belly up onto a table. Then you'll be asked to pull your waistband down. If your ultrasound technician is nice, she'll squirt some warm gel on your abdomen. If she's not so nice, she'll pull out the bottle of gel that's been chilling in the freezer for the past hour. I've had both kinds. I highly recommend the former. This sticky nasty gel is needed because otherwise the ul-

I wonder how many women involuntarily pee while getting an ultrasound.

trasound wouldn't be yucky enough.

After your belly has been lubed up with the extrahold hair gel, the technician will move a small transducer that looks like a computer mouse over your abdominal area. Actually, let me rephrase here. She doesn't so much move the transducer over your abdomen as she pushes really, really hard on your abdomen. When your belly actually touches your spine, she knows that she's pushing down hard enough. It's especially wonderful when she pushes down on your overfull bladder. As she pushes, the urine has two choices. It can back up to your eyes or it can come out. I wonder how many women involuntarily pee while getting an ultrasound.

That's not quite as bad as the method they use for ultrasounds early on in pregnancy, however. If you're very newly pregnant and need an ultrasound, the technician will hand you this probe and ask you to insert it.

"Insert it?" you'll ask, confused.

"Yes, insert it vaginally. The uterus is still very low in early pregnancy and we can get a better look this way."

"Oh that sounds great. This isn't going to be awkward at all."

I have a friend who asked the technician if the probe at least vibrated.

While the technician administers the test, you will crane your head around until you have a cramp in your neck, attempting to get a glimpse at the monitor. On occasion, I've had a technician who was nice enough to angle the monitor in my direction so I didn't have to turn my head around like an owl to see. Of course, it really doesn't matter whether you can clearly see the screen or not because you will have no clue what on earth you're looking at.

"Do you know what that is?" the technician will ask you, while pointing to a corner of the screen.

"Ummm, scrambled eggs and a short stack of pancakes?"

"No, silly! That's your baby's arm!"

"Ohhhh," you'll say, nodding your head like you can really make out the arm. In reality, it looks more like a map of Tallahassee.

"Look here! There's your baby's face!"

You squint. You close one eye. You tilt your head the other way and you see what looks a little like an alien.

The technician may ask you if you want to know the baby's sex. Unless you're one of those weird people who wants to be surprised, you emphatically shout, "YES!"

If you're lucky, Baby will cooperate and give the technician a nice butt shot. Then the ultrasound tech will say something like, "Awwww, see that? Ohhh. Are you excited?"

"See what? I don't know what I'm looking at! Is it a boy or a girl? Boy or girl! What is it???!" you bellow, while shaking the technician's shoulders.

Or maybe it's just me that does that. Hmmm . . .

My sister is one of those weird people. She wanted to be surprised with both of her pregnancies. I begged her to let me go to her ultrasound exam with her so the technician could tell me what she was having. I promised not to tell her, but she didn't go for it. She likes surprises. I, on the other hand, hate surprises, even if they're good surprises. I want to know and I want to know *now*. Better yet, I want to know yesterday! Besides, when you opt to find out your baby's sex on their actual birthday, you'll have a closet full of yellow and green clothes for your baby because that's what people buy you for shower gifts when you don't know if you're having a boy or a girl. And then when you take your newborn baby out in public, you'll have to constantly answer the question, "Is it a boy or a girl?" because, let's face it, babies all look pretty much alike, and the only way you can tell if a baby is a boy or a girl is by the little pink dress or blue overalls.

When I was pregnant with my first baby, I was desperate to know if I was having a boy or a girl as soon as humanly possible. My husband, however, wanted to be surprised. I know! He's one of *those* weirdos. Anyway, I informed my husband that since I was the one with the heartburn, swollen ankles, and stretch marks, it was only fair that I got my way and got to find out my baby's sex at the ultrasound. I promised him that I'd keep it a secret from him, however. Since Joe knows me and knew that I'd be able to keep it a secret for a maximum of three and a half minutes, he relented and decided to find out along with me at the ultrasound exam.

> Since I was the one with the heartburn, swollen ankles, and stretch marks, it was only fair that I got my way.

I was convinced I was having a girl, so I was thrown for a loop when the technician told me I was pregnant with a little boy.

It took me about an hour to adjust to this news because I'd been so sure I was carrying a girl. As the news sunk in, however, I was overjoyed with the idea of having a baby boy.

Being the wonderful, sweet, sacrificial woman I am, I let Joe have his way when I was pregnant with my second baby and told him we could wait until I gave birth to find out the sex of our baby. I duct-taped my mouth shut at the ultrasound so I wouldn't blurt out any questions about Baby's sex, and we ended up being surprised at the delivery. Not knowing nearly killed me. He still owes me for that one!

When I got pregnant with my third, I think the first thing I told Joe after letting him know I was pregnant was that it was *my* turn again, and we were going to learn the sex of the baby at the ultrasound whether he liked it or not. No more waiting for me, thankyouverymuch!

I was supernaturally nice when I got pregnant with my fourth baby, and I did the unthinkable—I told Joe that I'd go along with him if he wanted to be surprised again. Fair is fair, right? Because we were trying to figure out where we were going to put all the kids and who was going to be sharing a bedroom with whom, Joe declined and told me that he actually wanted to find out ahead of time so we could redo the kids' rooms. Yay, I thought! Bonus! I'm getting my way again! Unfortunately my baby didn't get that memo and was very uncooperative during the ultrasound exam. She wouldn't uncross her legs even once so we could get a peek, so we ended up being surprised after all.

With both my fifth and sixth babies, Joe and I agreed

to find out the sex at the ultrasound, and they both cooperated so we knew we were having a boy and a girl, respectively, before they were born. Of course, since our first four babies went boy, girl, boy, girl, we kind of expected to have a boy for our fifth and then another girl for our sixth, and that's exactly what happened. When people ask me how I managed to have my babies boy, girl, boy, girl, boy, girl, I usually answer them with, "I planned it that way." I just like watching the puzzled looks that cross their faces when I say that.

During the ultrasound exam, some hospitals will give you photos or even a DVD of your little one. Then you can take them home and quiz everyone on what exactly it is that they're looking at. If you're lucky, someone will be able to tell you what that gray blob next to that other gray blob is.

And finally, you'd think the best part of having an ultrasound is the assurance that everything looks like it's developing normally with your baby. Don't get me wrong, that is a wonderful, wonderful feeling. There's something about seeing your developing baby on the screen that just makes it all real. Shhh, don't tell anyone, but I cried at every single one of my ultrasounds. It's when I first realized that I was actually, indeed, for real, no stopping, no turning back, pregnant. But it isn't the best part of the ultrasound. The best part of having an ultrasound is getting to pee when you're done. Be prepared to pee for a good five minutes. Niagara Falls has nothing on a woman emptying her bladder after an obstetrical ultrasound. Ahhh . . .

Just Pee ~~in~~ Near This Cup

Another test you'll have repeatedly throughout your pregnancy is a urine test. At your first visit, your doctor will probably want to do a urinalysis and check for miscellaneous medical stuff. That's the technical term. Later on, he'll check your urine at every visit for signs of protein, which could indicate the serious problem of preeclampsia. Fortunately, by catching the possibility of preeclampsia early on with this urine test, doctors can manage it before it becomes a real problem.

This is a simple enough test. All the nurse will do is dip a specially treated paper into the cup of urine and examine the colored lines on the paper. All you have to do is pee in a cup. Easy enough, right? One would think.

It actually is a piece of cake for your first couple visits. However, as your belly grows, so does the difficulty of actually peeing *in* the cup. By the time you're nine months pregnant and have a belly the size of Utah, it's physically impossible to reach around your abdomen and get the cup anywhere near your butt. At this point, just pee in the toilet, then scoop a little toilet water into the cup when you're done. You might not want to use this method if your doctor's office uses those deodorizing tablets that turn the toilet water blue. Unless the nurse hasn't had any coffee yet and is a little hypnotized by looking at pregnant women's pee all day long, she's

> As your belly grows, so does the difficulty of actually peeing *in* the cup.

bound to notice your urine is blue. Otherwise, go for it! Yes, your test results will undoubtedly be strange, but it's better than peeing all over your hand, the toilet seat, your pants, and the floor. Not that that's ever happened to me or anything. I'm just saying . . .

Oftentimes, your doctor will ask for first morning urine for the same reason you needed to use first morning urine when you took your home pregnancy test—it's magical. The doctor will give you a cup to fill at home so you can bring the magical first morning urine in to your appointment later in the day. After filling the cup, you're supposed to put it in the refrigerator to keep it fresh, I guess. This is not a big deal when it's your first baby. If, however, you have other young children at home who like to help themselves to apple juice from the fridge, it could cause some issues.

As you drive to the office, you need to set your pee cup somewhere so it won't spill. Your car's built-in cup holders are perfect for this! Gross, yes, but handy. It's okay because it's got a top that screws on securely so you don't have to worry about mistakenly picking it up, thinking it's your double mocha half-caf iced latte. When it's time for your appointment, you have to hide your pee cup as you go into the office. I'm not sure why this is since at least half the people there have their own pee cups, but I'm telling you, you have to do it, probably for the same reason you have to hide your underwear in your jeans while you have an internal exam. You don't want to look like a freak who walks in just holding a cup of pee in plain sight of everyone else. You have two options for hiding your cup. You can put it in your purse, which might seem like a good idea at first, but let me explain. Sometimes those cups leak. Enough said. Or you can put it in a discreet paper bag and have people wonder if you've got a pint of malt liquor or a pee cup in the bag. I recommend the latter.

Just Drink This Sugar

The ultrasound is a breeze compared to the glucose-tolerance test. I think most doctors make you get this test done at some point during your pregnancy. This test is to ~~make you sick to your stomach~~ determine if you're developing gestational diabetes. Gestational diabetes is not an uncommon problem and can usually be managed quite well with diet and rest. My doctors always liked to do this test when I was around twenty weeks pregnant. With my last baby, because I was officially "old," my doctor insisted I have a glucose-tolerance test when I was six weeks pregnant and then again at twenty weeks. Extra fun for Dawn!

It's a simple test really, but you should be prepared for it. The test starts with you drinking this sugary beverage. It tastes sort of like orange pop with a five-pound bag of sugar, twenty-three packets of Splenda, and a gallon of high-fructose corn syrup added to it. So, you chew this drink and try to keep it down despite your stomach's desperate attempts to put it in reverse while you wait one hour to have your blood drawn. Although

> Try really, really hard not to throw up, or the mean technicians will make you drink another cup.

the drink is disgusting, try really, really hard not to throw up, or the mean technicians will make you drink another cup of it. I don't want to scare everyone about this test, so I'll tell you that I do have one friend who liked the drink. I'm lying through my teeth, but doesn't it make you feel better to think there are women out there who like it?

Anyway, you down this putrid concoction and then you wait. And wait. And wait. Now, the waiting really isn't so bad if this is your first baby or you have kids at home and you're getting a little break from them. You can read a couple magazines, crochet a baby blanket, or close your eyes and doze off. If you have your kids with you, however, it's another story. I've had to bring my children with me for this test on numerous occasions. It is not fun trying to occupy a baby and a couple toddlers in a small waiting room for an hour, especially if you're feeling a little woozy from drinking your weight in sucrose. If you need to bring young children with you, make sure you bring some coloring books and crayons so the kids can color for fifty-four seconds before getting bored, trying to eat the crayons, or throwing them around the waiting room. Snacks are a good thing to pack for the kids, but don't be tempted to eat any of them, despite the fact that your stomach is churning from the sugar-drink you just choked down. If you end up sneaking a granola bar from the kids, you'll screw up your blood-test results and you'll need to come back and take the test again. I always tried to talk my kids into playing the fun-filled game Let's Take a Nap while waiting to have my blood drawn. They almost never went for it, though. And in case you were wondering, it's not a good idea for you to play this game while your kids run around the waiting room like howler monkeys with attention deficit disorder. Just sayin' . . .

As crazy as it was trying to occupy my kids for an hour while waiting for the test, the worst glucose-tolerance test I remember was my very first one—before I even had any other children. I had to sit in a hot, crowded waiting room while taking the test. The patient sitting next to me must have just eaten a field of garlic and was daring to breathe. It was awful. Morning sickness, sugary drink, hot waiting room, garlic breath . . . Let's just say this is how I know they will make you drink the concoction again if you throw up.

After an hour of waiting, the technician will draw your blood. I think they look to see that the concentration is 2 percent blood cells and 98 percent sugar. Or something like that. Again, I'm not a doctor. I just play one on my computer. You really want to pass this test. Not only do you want to pass because it means you aren't showing signs of gestational diabetes, but because if you don't pass it, you'll most likely have to return and take a three-hour test.

The Test with the Four-Foot Needle

Because I was slightly on the oldish side when I was pregnant with Brooklyn, my doctor urged me to have genetic counseling and amniocentesis. Amniocentesis is a test where a doctor takes a four-foot needle and inserts it into your abdomen to withdraw some amniotic fluid for examination. I admit I never actually had amniocentesis done; however, I did have a consultation visit with a genetic counselor. When

I sat down in her office, she immediately began drilling me with questions:

"Do you know what your chances are of having a baby with a chromosomal defect?"

"Yes, well, my obstetrician mentioned that I'm at increased risk."

"And how likely are you to have a child with a chromosomal abnormality?" she demanded of me.

"Umm, I don't remember the actual number," I stammered.

"Then you don't know, do you!" she proclaimed triumphantly. She went on to cite numbers and statistics designed to make me sick with worry. Finally, she ended by insisting I have amniocentesis done to rule out any chromosomal abnormalities.

I refused. My reason for refusing was simply that I was not going to terminate my pregnancy if the test showed some problem. If we were blessed with a baby who had some abnormalities, then so be it. I was positive it would all work out and be okay in the end, whether the baby was perfectly normal or had some special issues. Because the results wouldn't change the course of my pregnancy, I opted not to have this invasive test.

Well, it was either that or the fact that I didn't really want a four-foot needle stuck into my abdomen.

Honestly, though, I have a few friends who did get amniocentesis done, and they all had the same thing to say about it: "It's not that bad. You exaggerate too much!" Truly, they all insisted the needle wasn't all that painful and the peace of mind it gave them was worth it. If you'll be over the age of thirty-five when you deliver your baby, your doctor will probably bring this test up to you. Or you could always lie about your age, which is what I'll do if I ever find myself pregnant again. Think I could pass for twenty-nine? Don't answer that!

Oh, I should mention that amniocentesis is not only used to determine the possibility of chromosomal defects. If you go into labor prematurely, you may need to have amniocentesis to help your doctors ascertain if the baby's lungs are mature enough to survive without intervention. A wealth of information can be garnered from the sampling of amniotic fluid, and the test shouldn't be automatically discounted if your physician really thinks you need it. Still, there are risks involved that you'll need to discuss with your doctor, and ultimately the decision is yours. Oh yeah, and my friends think it's necessary I tell you that the needle is not, in actuality, four feet long.

The Non-Stress Test (Really, It Isn't Stressful!)

I have no idea why they felt the need to use the word *stress* in regards to a pregnancy-related test. It's just mean, I tell ya! But this test really is nonstressful. Is that a word? I don't know, but really, the test won't stress you out. Generally, non-stress tests (NSTs) are given late in pregnancy and are a noninvasive way to check on Baby's well-being. When you have an NST, you will need to go to the hospital, your doctor's office, or a medical facility of some sort. All the NSTs

I had done during my pregnancies were done in a hospital.

I remember having a non-stress test done when I was pregnant with my fifth baby, Clayton. They had me lie down on a hospital bed while they hooked up a couple monitors. The nurse squirted some gel on my abdomen—because every pregnancy test includes the use of gel—and then she placed two small sensors about the size of a computer mouse, on my belly. Next, she pulled out a couple elastic belts that were long enough to stretch around the equator one and a half times because that's about how big my belly was. One sensor monitors the baby's heartbeat, and the other one monitors any contractions you may be having. (These are the same monitors you'll have on during labor if you deliver at a typical hospital.) This is probably the best test you'll ever have because your only job during the test is to lie back and relax. That's it. The sensors will pick up information about contractions and Baby's heartbeat, and it will be displayed on a screen and/or printed out on a paper. You'll probably be given a little button to push every time you feel the baby move. When you push the button, it will leave a little mark on the paper printout. The nurses will look to see that Baby's heart rate rises every time a mark on the paper is seen. This button looks like a buzzer that contestants on a game show might use. While you're lying there resting, I suggest you turn to *Jeopardy* on the TV; and every time you know an answer, push the button before the other contestants do. It's fun. When the nurse comes in to check on you and sees all sorts of random marks on the paper from where you went crazy pushing the button, tell her you just won the Daily Double and she'll understand.

If Baby's heart rate doesn't react like it should or your baby isn't moving much, they may give you some juice or a snack to see if

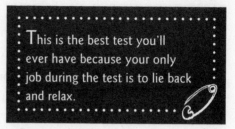

This is the best test you'll ever have because your only job during the test is to lie back and relax.

that wakes up Baby a little. They always gave me graham crackers and orange juice. I tried to get the nurses to bring me a cheeseburger once, but was informed it wasn't a hotel with room service. Hey, it doesn't hurt to ask. Nothing ventured, nothing gained, right?

If you aren't due yet and the NST shows that you're having frequent, regular contractions, you may need to stay for further evaluation. This may sound bad, but believe me, after you already have one or more kids, this is heavenly! You get to lie around in bed, watching TV or reading or sleeping, and not once will you have to get up and pull the toddler off the kitchen counter or change the baby's poopy diaper or remind your seven-year-old that the squirrel he just caught needs to stay outside.

I had to stay for further evaluation with Clayton. I started having contractions when I was about seven months along. My NST showed that I was having regular contractions, so my doctor had the nurse give me an IV of fluids to see if extra hydration would stop the contractions. It didn't make a difference, so I was given a shot of ~~poison~~ medication in my IV in an effort to stop the contractions. This drug made me feel horrible. I had heart palpitations and felt dizzy and nauseous. It felt almost like it does when I walk into the kids' rooms and see that they've colored on their walls with permanent marker. Still, the medicine worked and stopped the contractions. After some monitoring, I was sent home and told to rest. Ha! You don't tell a mother of four to rest unless you're offering to come babysit for her. I have yet to hear a doctor offer to do that.

Another time you may have an NST is when your baby is overdue. I was sent for several NSTs for my first four babies because they were all overdue. My doctor tortured me by making me come to the hospital, where I could see all the pregnant women walking around the maternity ward. She coldheartedly reminded me that I was only there for a test and would soon be sent home again, even though my baby had been due four days earlier. If you end up needing a non-stress test, don't worry about it—it's a NON-stress test. Kick back and pretend you're in a hotel chillin' and relaxin' with an assortment of belts and monitors and computer printouts surrounding you. Just don't try to order a cheeseburger from the nurse.

The "Do You Weigh More Than an Elephant?" Test

I think the most painful test you'll have while pregnant is not really a test at all. It's getting weighed. Your doctor will weigh you at every visit ~~to humiliate you~~ so he can make sure you and Baby are healthy. Or maybe he does it because they have an office pool and they take bets on just how big you're going to get. Or maybe it's so he can scold you if you eat your weight in chocolate chip cookies.

Before weighing in at every visit, I did everything in my power to make sure the scale didn't tip too far toward the point of no return. I tried to wear the lightest-weight clothing I owned, even if it was in the dead of winter. I took off my shoes before stepping on the scale every time. I emptied my pockets and made sure I wasn't adding cell-phone or car-key weight to my total. I ~~went to ridiculous lengths~~ performed a perfectly reasonable and acceptable ritual before weighing in, which included going to the bathroom, blowing my nose, exfoliating, trimming my nails, and tweezing my eyebrows. Every hundredth of an ounce counts, you know.

All I know is that I gained sixty-five pounds with my first baby. I had an attitude of, "Oh, well, I'm pregnant! I can eat whatever I want! I'm pregnant, you know!" Only I wasn't eating for two. I was eating for five or six or twenty-seven. Of course, it didn't help that I had cravings for less-than-nutritious, high-calorie food all the time, either. And, because of my morning sickness, I ended up eating a lot of carbs—crackers, bread, pasta—because that's what settled my stomach more than anything.

The thing is, if you gain too much weight, losing it after Baby is born will be that much harder. As much as we'd like to think we're going to lose sixty pounds when Baby is born, human babies don't usually weight quite that much at birth. Yikes, that would make for one painful delivery if they did! By the

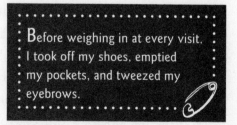

Before weighing in at every visit, I took off my shoes, emptied my pockets, and tweezed my eyebrows.

time I stopped breast-feeding my firstborn at nine months, I was pregnant again and there went all hope of losing my pregnancy weight. Thankfully I learned my lesson and kept my second pregnancy weight gain to a more moderate thirty pounds. I have yet to lose that sixty-pound weight gain from my first pregnancy fifteen years ago. Wow, that's depressing. Hmmm, let me ~~just lie about that~~ rephrase that. I'm almost back to my prepregnancy weight! Just a few more pounds to go! Now doesn't that sound better?

Pump It Up

Another thing you'll have monitored at each visit is your blood pressure. This test is not a big deal. The nurse will wrap a cuff around your arm and pump up her little squeezy thing until all feeling is cut off in your arm. Your fingers will turn blue and tingle. Then she will put her stethoscope in her ears and pretend like she's listening to your arm scream in pain, while she's really listening to Awesome 80s on her iPod. After a minute, she'll release the cuff, at which point blood will rush back into your hand. Then she'll pump it up again because nurses never, ever, ever get your blood pressure on the first try. When she's done listening to her tunes, she'll make some notes in your chart. What she's writing is a secret. Don't even ask to see it because she won't show you. It's probably her grocery list. As long as your blood pressure is okay, this test is not a problem. If your blood pressure starts to rise (I mean, more than it ordinarily does when you're at the doctor's office), you'll be monitored more frequently because high blood pressure is nothing to mess around with.

I generally have pretty low blood pressure. It's usually a good thing unless I try to stand up too quickly, in which case it sometimes makes me nearly fall back over. I remember one time at the doctor's office. I don't remember who I was pregnant with, but I know I had three kids with me for this particular appointment. They were bored and kept tossing My Little Ponies around the office, playing with the stirrups, and opening the drawers where the doctor keeps her ~~devices of torture~~ medical implements. They repeatedly climbed onto the step stool and jumped off while flapping their arms. I kept thinking, *Oh well, at least we're at a doctor's office in a medical building. There's bound to be someone here who can treat a broken arm when one of them falls.* They opened and closed the garbage can again and again because it's fun to pick up germs at the doctor's office like that.

By the time the doctor came in, my blood pressure was through the ceiling. I insisted it would come down if she took the kids out of the office. She didn't offer to babysit for me, but my blood pressure did indeed come down eventually. So, just because you have an elevated reading one time, don't go freaking out. Your blood pressure can fluctuate some, especially if you're trying to listen to your doctor while keeping flying plastic ponies from hitting her in the head.

The Worst Things
About Being Pregnant

. . . .

1. Instead of looking at your face, people focus on your belly when talking to you.

2. Feeling like a turtle stuck on its back when trying to get out of bed

3. Strangers coming up to you and touching your belly

4. Being unable to reach around your belly or bend over far enough to shave your legs or trim your toenails

5. Peeing on your hand while trying to fill the cup at every doctor's appointment

6. Heartburn

7. Aching back

8. Varicose veins

9. Morning sickness

10. Fatigue of epic proportions

CHAPTER 4

IN THE BEGINNING

(MONTH ONE)

F irst a quick note on months. Everyone says that a typical pregnancy lasts nine months. But when you actually count the weeks, you think, *Hey! It's more like ten months! What's up with that?!* First off, take heart. It could be worse. An African elephant is pregnant for twenty-two months. TWENTY-TWO months! That's almost two years! And not only that, their babies weigh about 260 pounds at birth. Talk about ouch!

A typical pregnancy lasts about forty weeks, give or take a week or two. When people count four weeks as a *month*, yes, pregnancy lasts about ten months. But there are rarely twenty-eight days in a month. So if you're talking calendar months, pregnancy lasts closer to nine months. The important thing to remember here is that no matter how you look at it, pregnancy lasts at least a good two months longer than we'd like it to last. Ask any woman who is seven months

YOU'LL LOSE THE BABY WEIGHT

pregnant and she'll tell you, "I'm ready!" I'll admit there is the occasional woman who boasts, "I could stay pregnant forever! I just *love* being pregnant." The best way to deal with Ms. I-Love-Being-Pregnant is to smile and say, "How wonderful for you." Then put a voodoo hex on her to have a colossally painful delivery.

Okay, back to the first month. You'll have a lot of questions when you first discover you're pregnant, especially if this is your first baby. You'll need to find a doctor you like and trust because you'll be spending quite a lot of time ~~sitting around in his waiting room~~ at his office. You'll certainly want to learn the best way to take care of yourself and your baby. Every newly pregnant woman has a ton of questions and concerns as she embarks on this exciting, new, and most important journey. Questions like, Do I have to give up drinking a pot of coffee every morning, and if I do, how will I ever make it through the day without falling asleep? Or, Can I continue to work throughout my pregnancy? And what on earth am I going to name this baby?

You may have more specific questions, such as, I just gave birth two months ago and I'm pregnant again. Is that bad? Or maybe, I just learned that I'm pregnant with my eighth baby. Does that pose more risk for me? Or, how can I use this pregnancy as an excuse to get out of doing housework? In this chapter, I'll go over some of the things you'll experience in the first month of pregnancy.

Choosing a Doctor Is Harder Than Finding a Husband!

One of the first things you'll need to do is find a doctor. Perhaps you've already got an ob/gyn that you love. If that's the case, count yourself lucky! A couple generations ago, women had an easier task of choosing a doctor because there weren't so many options. There might have been a couple doctors from which they could choose; but in the end, it probably didn't matter who they picked, because women were generally put out with anesthesia to give birth. They weren't even awake and aware, so it didn't much matter who delivered their baby. My mom grew up in such a small town that the local OB was also the town's veterinarian. Okay, maybe that's a slight exaggeration, but really, there were no fancy birthing centers, no one dreamed of giving birth to their babies underwater, and there weren't dozens of doctors to choose from.

In your search for a physician today, you'll want to keep a few things in mind. What kind of birthing experience would you like? Are you more comfortable in a sterile hospital setting, surrounded by medical equipment and the latest technology? Perhaps your idea of the perfect birthing experience takes place in your home surrounded by your family. Or maybe you fantasize about giving birth in an airplane or while scuba diving or in a tree house, in which case what is wrong with

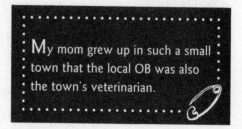

My mom grew up in such a small town that the local OB was also the town's veterinarian.

you??? you may be hard-pressed to find a doctor willing to work with you.

I personally liked giving birth in a hospital setting. I felt comfortable being surrounded by beeping machines and plenty of nurses. I would never even consider giving birth at home. I could just imagine how that scenario would play out! The kids would be barging into my room every five minutes to inform me of stuff: "Clay's climbing on the kitchen table. Mom, Lexi isn't wearing her glasses!" They'd bombard me with a constant stream of questions like, "Can I go to John's house? Will you get me some chocolate milk? Mom, what time is my baseball game at? Can you make us tacos for dinner?" And my dear husband would undoubtedly be watching TV in the other room and insist, "I didn't realize the kids were bothering you. Sorry."

I guess I don't think there's anything wrong with giving birth at home if that's your kind of thing, but I always looked forward to getting away from my home and the other kids for a couple days. Why do you think I have so many kids? That was my way of getting a little vacation! What can I say? Some people plan their vacations for Disney World. I planned mine for the hospital. And in the hospital, I felt assurance that the medical professionals could handle any situation should an emergency arise. That was just my preference. Because of that, I chose an obstetrician and gave birth in the birthing center at a big hospital.

If, however, you want to feel more in control of your childbirth experience, you might want to consider a certified nurse-midwife. Generally, certified nurse-midwives will take more time to talk with and listen to you. They will treat you more as a *person* than as a *patient*. Certified nurse-midwives tend to veer more toward natural childbirth. If you feel strongly about avoiding any unnecessary medical intervention, then a nurse-midwife may be the way to go for you. That's not to say that you can't have a certified nurse-midwife if you're the kind of person who orders her epidural the minute she gets a positive pregnancy test, however. Or that you can't have an obstetrician at a big-city hospital who will help to make your childbirth experience as natural as possible.

Also, take into consideration whether the doctor you choose is in practice by himself or with partners. If he's by himself, you'll probably see him at every visit and he'll be the one to deliver your baby. Unless, of course, he's on vacation when you deliver and you know, with Murphy's Law, that will be the way it works. In that case you may have to see whoever is filling in for him, and it will probably be a doctor you've never met. If your doctor is part of a group, you'll most likely have to see every doctor in the group at least once throughout your pregnancy, and you won't get much say in who delivers your baby. The good news is you'll have at least met the doctor who delivers your baby. The bad news is it could be the one doctor in the group you really, really don't like. And that's the law with groups—there must be one doctor out of the half dozen or so that you don't care for.

That happened to me with my sixth baby. I really liked all the doctors in the practice except one. He annoyed me. I wanted to slap him. The first time I saw him, he commented on the amount of weight I'd gained. Strike one.

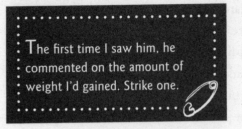

The first time I saw him, he commented on the amount of weight I'd gained. Strike one.

Later, I told a joke and he didn't laugh. What kind of boring person doesn't laugh at my jokes? Strike two. Did I mention that he commented on my weight gain? Strike three. Of course, he was the one who ended up delivering my baby. What can you do? Nothing.

The obstetrician who delivered my first four babies was in practice by herself. She delivered every one of those children. She was a tiny, petite Indian woman who could barely see over the steering wheel of her car. Poor Joe could never understand a word she said with her thick accent.

"Would you like to cut the umbilical cord?" she'd ask him.

"Oh no thanks, I've already eaten."

"So what are you going to name this baby?" she'd inquire as she handed the baby to Joe.

"Oh, it's ten thirty," he'd answer, not having a clue what she'd just asked him.

I not only loved my doctor, but I also loved the hospital she was at for the first three babies I had. She moved offices and affiliations when I was pregnant with my fourth baby, however. I followed her to the new office and new hospital, but I had such an awful experience and disliked that hospital so very much that I ended up switching doctors after Lexi, my fourth baby, was born. Actually, saying I disliked the hospital is a ~~huge~~ mild understatement. Unless I get in a life-or-death car wreck right outside its doors, I refuse to set foot in that hospital ever again. My nurses were mean and one of them yelled at me and threatened to take my new baby away from me if I didn't nurse her more often. I calmly and politely replied, "Hello? She's my *fourth* baby! I *know* what I'm doing, and you most certainly will NOT take her away from me!" She left in a huff and didn't bother me again.

The miniblinds over the windows in my bathroom were broken, and my window viewed another tower of hospital rooms. The poor patients who looked out those windows probably saw a little more than they'd cared to see. Watching a woman who has just given birth try to poop could scar anyone for life. And, of course, I'd been spoiled by the beautiful new birthing center where I'd delivered my first three babies. I decided that I never wanted to deliver another baby at that facility. Ever.

That brings me to another point: Although I think it's important to have a physician you like and trust, I also think it's a good thing to check out the hospital or birthing center where you'll deliver, ahead of time. Check out your first choice and make sure they have all the amenities you want—room service, a hot tub, minibar, etc. Most places offer tours for expectant parents. Schedule a tour early in your pregnancy if your facility offers that. My obstetrician was great, but I was so disappointed in the hospital, the nurses, and my room that I searched for a new doctor when I learned I was pregnant with my fifth baby. I know you'll be in the hospital for only a couple days and maybe it shouldn't matter too much, but it does. The hospital room, rules, and especially staff can really make your delivery an awesome experience or an experience that makes you want to take your new baby and run from the hospital screaming. Because I'm basically a lazy person, one of the biggest draws to the birthing center was the fact that I never had to change rooms. I labored, delivered, recovered, and spent the entirety of my stay in the same room. And that room was furnished with lovely wood floors, a whirlpool tub, and a refrigerator, which played very well into my whole "vacation at the hospital" idea.

You (or more specifically, your partner) may want to make a test run or two as well. You know, see how long it takes to load up the suitcase and drive to the hospital in regular conditions, at rush hour, through construction, or during a snowstorm.

You'll want to make sure the doctors you choose accepts your insurance. If they don't, you could wind up like my friend Amy, who had to make monthly payments and didn't own her daughter free and clear until she was three years old.

Also, whatever physician you choose, you want to make sure they listen to you and take your questions and concerns seriously. Make a list of questions you have during the days and weeks before your appointment and bring them with you to discuss. Don't rely on your brain to remember stuff because the new little baby growing inside you will suck your brain cells right out of your head and you will, without a doubt, suffer from "baby brain." (I'll talk about baby brain more in depth later because this subject deserves a section of its own.) You won't remember a thing and you'll do stuff like wander around looking for your shoes that you put in the bathtub for some reason, and walk into a room and promptly forget what you were going to get. Make a list!

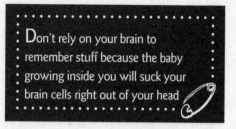

Don't rely on your brain to remember stuff because the baby growing inside you will suck your brain cells right out of your head

And the caregiver you choose should welcome your questions and take time to discuss them no matter how ~~stupid they are~~ silly you think they might be. You should never feel stupid calling them with a concern. That's what they're there for. That's why you've hired them to care for you and your baby. That's why you're paying them. If they make you feel like you're wasting their time with your questions, remind them that you're the one helping to finance their kids' college education.

When You're ~~Old~~ at an "Advanced Maternal Age"

When I went to the doctor for my first appointment with my sixth pregnancy, the nurse took one look at my chart and said, "Oh, I see you'll be thirty-six when you have this baby."

"Yep," I replied, completely clueless to what lay ahead.

"Oh," she said, shaking her head. She made some notes in my chart, looked up at me, then went back to scribbling.

"What's wrong?" I asked, starting to get worried.

"Well, ~~you're really very OLD~~ obstetrically speaking, you're at an advanced maternal age."

"Advanced maternal age?" I inquired. I just had a baby

about a year ago and no one said anything about *advanced maternal age.* Did I age *that* much in the past year?

Then she said it was a wonder I'd even been able to conceive, what with me being so old and all. She laughed at me and said, "Wow, you're going to be superold by the time this baby gets into high school!"

Okay, so maybe she didn't really say those things, but that's what I was thinking. Right off the bat, the nurse informed me that I'd need extra obstetrical care and more tests and would probably be eligible for the senior discount at Wendy's and an AARP card by the time the baby was born.

"You're at an increased risk for gestational diabetes, so you'll need to take two glucose-tolerance tests this pregnancy."

"Oh fun!" I cried. "They're my favorite!" I gushed, sarcasm dripping from my every word.

"You'll also need to have amniocentesis and/or a level three ultrasound done."

"Amniohuh?" I stopped goofing off when I thought of having a twenty-foot needle jammed into my belly.

She continued with, "You're about four thousand times more likely to have problems with your pregnancy or a baby with a genetic defect than a younger mother."

Now thankfully, I'd already had five babies and had been through the whole pregnancy and childbirth thing before, so I took her dire predictions with a grain of salt. Had this been my first child, however, I probably would've dissolved in a puddle of tears right then and there.

I'll tell it like it is here so you don't have to be scared.

It's not all doom and gloom if you're at an "advanced maternal age." There is good news. Yes it's true that the older the mother,

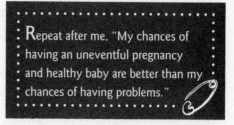

Repeat after me, "My chances of having an uneventful pregnancy and healthy baby are better than my chances of having problems."

the more chances there are of complications or problems. Still, the chances of you having a healthy baby and healthy pregnancy are way more *for* you than against you. Sure, you might have to have an extra test or two, but it's just because ~~you have better insurance than younger mothers~~ your doctor is looking out for you. Seriously, repeat after me, "My chances of having an uneventful pregnancy and healthy baby are better than my chances of having problems." There. That's better, don't you think?

I'm not sure why, but apparently the cutoff time is thirty-five years old. Once you hit that mark, you're old. I guess they have to draw the line somewhere, and thirty-five is it. Nowadays, it's not at all uncommon for a woman to be having her first child at age thirty-five or thirty-eight or forty-two. With advances in reproductive technology and increased medical care, women can rest assured that the odds of having a normal, uncomplicated pregnancy and healthy baby are absolutely in their favor.

If you happen to fall into this "advanced maternal age" bracket, be prepared for an extra test or two. Then relax. After all, in the Bible, Sarah gave birth to Isaac at the ripe old age of ninety, and they didn't even have ultrasounds back then.

Save the Alcohol for When the Baby's a Toddler

Some other concerns you may have when you first find out you're pregnant are about taking care of yourself. What if you did something that wasn't totally healthy before you found out you were pregnant?

I suppose most women try to give up any harmful habits like smoking or drinking alcohol when they start trying to conceive. Other people, like me, who don't actually plan these things and wake up one day suddenly pregnant may find themselves worrying that something they did might have somehow harmed their baby.

On more than one occasion, I had a couple glasses of wine before I knew I was pregnant. This happened to several of my friends as well. There were a couple times when I'd taken some Advil before learning I was pregnant. I have a friend who had taken strong cold medicine for a week before realizing she was pregnant. Not to mention the times you had X-rays, went skydiving, rode a roller-coaster, played with plutonium, or rappelled down the side of the Eiffel Tower. These are things you probably wouldn't do if you knew you were pregnant.

Relax. It happens. In fact, it happens a lot. The good news is, this early in pregnancy, there's no evidence that a couple drinks on a couple occasions before you realized you were pregnant will do any harm. The important thing is to stop once you find out you're pregnant. Really, you'll want to save the alcohol for when your baby is a toddler and paints his room with the contents of his dirty diaper.

And don't worry about the ibuprofen you took before you knew you were pregnant; just don't automatically grab the pain relievers when you get a headache anymore. Instead, get used to the idea that as a mom, you're just going to have to deal with the pain and keep going. It's good practice for when you have a splitting migraine and yet your daughter has to practice her violin—the violin she's had for only three months, the violin that causes all the stray cats in the neighborhood to howl at your window, *that* violin.

Honey, Get the Cat Box

Here's a little bonus for you newly pregnant ladies. You have a valid excuse not to change the litter box anymore! For real. Honestly, this isn't like the time I said I couldn't change the toddler's diapers. It's not like the time I told my husband that I was under strict doctor's orders not to cook dinner anymore. And it's definitely not like the time I told everyone that I needed to eat ice cream every night for my well-being. This is for real. Cats can transmit toxoplasmosis, and that would be bad to get. I didn't just make this up. Really, look it up! Toxoplasmosis is a real thing. I have no idea what it is, how you get it, or what it can do to you, but if you have a cat, ask your caregiver about it. And then tell your husbands, boyfriends, roommates, or kids the cat box duty is theirs for the next nine months.

I Think We Need to Hire a Housekeeper

Although I don't believe there's any evidence that cleaning your house is bad for you during pregnancy, I think you should pretend it is. Enlist your husband's help with this chore. It may not hurt you to scrub the bathrooms, but the smell of bleach makes me woozy when I'm not pregnant, so I think I'd probably get faint and/or throw up if I was. And if I threw up in the bathroom while I was cleaning it, it would just make it even messier and, really, who needs that? I say, let the cleaning slide. Once your baby arrives, you won't have time to clean anyway. Use your pregnancy as a chance to get used to the mess of having kids and/or as a way of introducing your husband or older kids to helping out around the house a little more.

Or, if you can afford it, you could even hire a housekeeper to come in and spruce things up a bit once or twice a month. Just don't act like me and think you have to clean before the cleaning lady comes so she won't think you're a slob. That just defeats the purpose of having a cleaning person.

And you'll probably want to paint the nursery. I'm pretty sure the safety of a pregnant woman painting went back and forth with each of my pregnancies. With my first, I heard it's not safe! Don't paint! With my second, it was fine and dandy; paint poses no risks. With my third, it was back to paint is

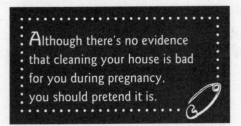

Although there's no evidence that cleaning your house is bad for you during pregnancy, you should pretend it is.

bad. By my fourth, it was okay again. The fifth—just say no to paint! The sixth—okie dokie. Okay, maybe I'm exaggerating a bit, but my theory is—when in doubt, make someone else do it. Really, take advantage of anyone's help with these chores, because it'll be a few years until you can ~~pass them off on Junior~~ teach Junior how to clean the bathroom and help out around the house.

The Dreaded "D" Word

I know, I know, but I just have to say it. Diet. Don't get all freaked out on me though. I don't mean diet as in, "you can only eat carrots and drink water" diet. I just mean diet as in, "be aware of what and how much you eat." In truth, my diet during pregnancy looked a little like this: eat whatever you want, whenever you want, and as much as you want, and do it with the excuse that you're eating for two.

"Oh sure, I'd love to go to Dairy Queen. Yes, I'm sure I want two banana split supremes. You know, because I'm eating for two. You know, since I'm pregnant. And the baby is hungry. And the baby is the one who is craving Dairy Queen. I'm only eating it for the baby. You know, because I'm pregnant." The fact that I gained about enough weight to give birth to a 260-pound baby elephant is irrelevant. The fact that I still haven't lost that weight despite the fact that my "baby" is now fifteen years old doesn't matter.

Hey, I never claimed to be a dietician. Seriously, though, pregnancy is not the time to lose weight or worry about how much you weigh or ~~if you'll ever~~ when you'll fit back into your skinny jeans. That said, you really should try to keep your weight gain to a moderate amount. I believe the going rate is twenty-five to thirty-five pounds these days, although that has changed a few times in the last forty years. Check with your doctor for his recommendations. You also want to make sure you get enough of the nutrients you need. For example:

* Dairy—a chocolate shake and half a pound of cheese should do the trick.
* Vegetables—a sixteen-ounce container of spinach dip will do nicely.
* Fruit—a quarter of a cheesecake topped with raspberry sauce fulfills your fruit requirement.
* Bread—a loaf of King's Hawaiian bread (you need something with which to eat the spinach dip) and a pound of butter cookies takes care of your bread requirement.
* Protein—sausage pizza, a big, fat hamburger, and twenty Reese's Peanut Butter Cups (What? Peanut butter has protein!) fills the need for protein.

Yep, looks like a well-rounded diet to me. And for lunch you can have . . .

Oh yeah, in case you don't get quite enough nutrients from that diet, make sure you take a prenatal vitamin every day. Your doctor should suggest or prescribe one at your first appointment. Actually, if you're not pregnant yet and you're just reading this book because you're an overachiever, start taking vitamins when you begin trying to conceive. You'll be healthy as a horse. (Are horses really all that healthy? What if it's a sick horse? Horses can get sick, can't they? And why is it a horse?

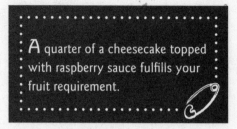

A quarter of a cheesecake topped with raspberry sauce fulfills your fruit requirement.

Why not a wombat? What if the saying was healthy as a wombat? Or a flying squirrel? I think I've discovered where my son got his ADD.) Anyway, you'll be as healthy as possible when you conceive. And you definitely want to get folic acid in your diet from the beginning, and it's just kinda fun to say "folic acid." I mean, usually acid is a bad thing, like "burned by acid" or "dropping acid" but in this case it's an essential vitamin-like thing. You need it. It can help keep your baby healthy. Hey, I don't make this stuff up. Trust me.

Must. Have. Coffee.

If you get out of bed and stumble around with your eyes closed while making monosyllabic grunts before you have your coffee, giving up caffeine can be a challenge. Sure, it's a good idea to give up caffeine when you're pregnant, but for some of us, it's hard. Like really, really hard. Like it might possibly be easier to give up breathing than our morning cuppa joe. If this is the case with you, I suggest cutting back on caffeine. Instead of drinking six cups of coffee in the morning, try staying awake on one or two. Or instead of the regular coffee you use, try making it with half decaf. Or perhaps try a cup of tea (which generally has less caffeine

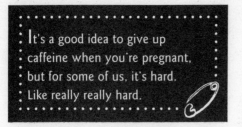

It's a good idea to give up caffeine when you're pregnant, but for some of us, it's hard. Like really really hard.

than coffee) instead of coffee.

If you can get by in the morning without coffee, but find it hard to make it through the day without a Diet Coke or two, again, try cutting down. Replace one of your usual caffeinated beverages with water or another caffeine-free substitute.

With my first pregnancy, I tried to give up caffeine completely. I tried, but I couldn't take the never-ending headaches. I thought I might be able to get beyond the headaches if I could just stick it out another couple weeks, but I just didn't have it in me. Besides, my coworkers were scared of the uncaffeinated version of me and begged me to ingest some coffee, pop, anything with a modicum of caffeine in it before my head actually imploded. I ended up just cutting back on my caffeine consumption instead of cutting out caffeine entirely and my coworkers eventually let me have my scissors back. So, my advice to you is, if you plan to give it up altogether, just wear a sign around your neck to give others fair warning. "I'm pregnant and I haven't had any coffee." People will see you coming and make a hasty retreat, which should avoid any unnecessary violence.

You're Pregnant Again?

What if this is your fifth or sixth or seventeenth child? Well, with increased pregnancies comes a slight increase in ~~insanity~~

risk. In reality, though, as long as you're getting good medical care, there's no reason why a mother on her sixth pregnancy won't have as good an outcome as a mother on her first. In fact, in many ways, I enjoyed my later pregnancies more than my first because I knew what to expect. I wasn't scared or nervous about every little thing. Actually, that's not entirely accurate. I was just too busy taking care of my other kids to notice much about my later pregnancies.

Of course, mothers of many do have a few additional factors to consider. Mothers of many tend to be a little older than your average first-time mother. This is because having children ages you. It exponentially ages you and turns you gray, so the more you have, the older you feel. Well, that and the fact that it takes nine months to have a baby, so it takes a few years to have six kids, which makes you a bit older than the average mom working on her first pregnancy.

Mothers who have given birth multiple times also tend to carry around a little extra weight. I can't imagine why. *Innocent whistling*. I know *I* never gained any extra weight that stayed on forever with any of *my* pregnancies. Ahem. If you're overweight, there may be an increased risk of gestational diabetes or other problems.

There is one increased risk when you're pregnant with your fifth or subsequent baby that makes me laugh. It's having multiples. Ironic, huh? Mother Nature's a funny one, all right. So if you're thinking that you'll have just one baby to make it an even half dozen, think again. You may just have two or three at once. I was certain that I was having twins when I was pregnant with my sixth baby. I just *knew* it would be twins and I'd end up with an odd number of

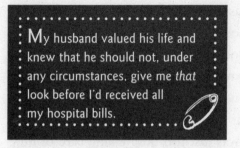

My husband valued his life and knew that he should not, under any circumstances, give me *that* look before I'd received all my hospital bills.

children and it would throw off the whole boy, girl, boy, girl, boy, girl thing I had going. Then what? I'd have to get pregnant again and have just one more so it was all evened out. And what if I had twins again? (Like I said at the beginning of this section, the more children you have, the crazier you get.)

I'm not really sure why the chances of having twins goes up for moms of many. Maybe it's because we tend to be a bit older, and the older you are, the higher the chance of releasing more than one egg. Maybe it's simply a numbers game. You have enough kids and eventually you're bound to get a set of twins in there somewhere. Or perhaps God just has a sense of humor.

Another kind of twins is Irish twins. Maybe the term *Irish twins* isn't politically correct, but you know what I'm talking about here—siblings born a year or less apart. I, for the life of me, cannot fathom how this could happen. There was *no* chance of me having babies nine months apart, that's for sure. My husband valued his life and knew that he should not, under any circumstances, give me *that* look before I'd even received all my hospital bills from my last delivery.

My friend Julie has babies who are eleven months apart. I still look at her like she's some sort of weirdo whenever I see her. When I found out she was pregnant again, I had to restrain myself from asking her, "Really? For real? How? WHY?"

Honestly, Julie and her husband had struggled with infertility for years. She conceived her first son with the aid of medical intervention. After he was born, the thought of using birth control never crossed her mind. Surprise! Her second son was conceived the old-fashioned way (and way too soon after giving birth to her first, if you ask me).

When my first baby was two months old, I was surviving on fifty-three minutes of sleep a night, I brushed my teeth with coffee, I was up to my elbows in poopy diapers, I hadn't lost an ounce of my pregnancy weight, and most days I couldn't even find the time to get in the shower. Oh yeah, clearly I was one irresistible babe back then. I don't know how my husband managed to control himself around my unshowered, tired crabbiness. And having another baby (or more specifically, the act that gets you to that point) was the last thing on my mind. To all of you with a set of Irish twins, all I can say is, what on earth were you thinking???

Achoo!

When you get sick while you're pregnant, you can't automatically go to the drugstore, pick up your favorite sickness cure-all, take it, and feel better. And as luck would have it, my friends and I got sick more often than ever while we were pregnant. I'm pretty sure it's a scientific fact that your immune system simply shuts down while you're pregnant. My theory is that the baby sucks all the vitamin C and germfighting goodness out of your body. We never got so many

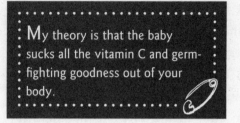

My theory is that the baby sucks all the vitamin C and germ-fighting goodness out of your body.

colds as we did while carrying our babies, which totally stinks because, like I said, you can't take any ole cold medicine to help you feel better.

Oh yes, there are some people out there who would have you believe that there are safe, effective, natural home remedies that work just as well as medication. They're fools. Let's see if I can remember some of those . . .

1. *Try to avoid getting sick in the first place. Wash your hands frequently.*

Well duh! Why didn't I think of that?! If we could avoid getting sick in the first place, no one would ever be sick! And of course you should wash your hands, but I say you should go one further. If you have little kids at home, capture them the instant they walk in the door from school and hose them down with Lysol. And grocery carts are just teeming with germs. Make someone else do the shopping for you for the duration of your pregnancy. Use your ongoing avoidance of germs as an excuse to get out of going to your in-laws' house for dinner. You must avoid all germs at all costs, you know, for the baby.

2. *Get plenty of rest and eat well.*

Ha-ha-ha-ha! Oh ouch! I think I pulled something laughing over this one!

3. *Use saline nose spray or a neti pot with a saline solution to help clear sinuses of congestion. It can help clear stuffy noses without drugs.*

Oh sure, what a great idea—pouring salt water up your nose on purpose. There's another word for this, you know. It's called DROWNING!

4. *For sore throats, try some nice hot tea with honey and lemon. It's very soothing.*

Uh-huh. Hot tea. Sure, that'll work. I have some better advice for you. Just try not to yell at your older kids too much. It will only make you lose your voice, and then you'll be completely powerless against them. The kids will take over the house, and there won't be a darn thing you'll be able to do about it. Your kids will just laugh at you as you make pitiful squeaking noises while attempting to yell at them to stop flinging marshmallows at the ceiling fan.

Chances are you'll develop a headache at some point in your pregnancy. For the first three months of all my pregnancies, I got frequent, painful headaches. If you should suffer from headaches also, just look at it this way—it's practice for when you've *had* kids and they run screaming through the house, fighting with one another.

Again, don't automatically reach for your favorite pain reliever. Ask your doctor for advice if you should experience headaches. Some nonmedicine things you can do to help alleviate the pain are lie down in a quiet, darkened room and place a cool washcloth on your head. I'm pretty sure this does nothing to help with the pain, but it makes you look like you're officially not feeling well, may garner sympathy from your husband, and may help prevent energetic kids from jumping all over you.

If you actually cough up a lung, are running a fever of 128, or your skin suddenly has rainbow polka dots, call your doctor. If your cold lasts more than a couple days, give your doctor a call. If your older kids all come down with strep throat and they share their germs with you, give your doctor a call. If you suspect an ear or sinus infection, you may need antibiotics, so give your doctor a ring. Basically, just call your doctor when you aren't feeling well and whine over the phone. While you're at it, call your parents, sister, husband, girlfriends, mailman, grocery store cashier, and your first-grade teacher and beg for sympathy. Whine profusely into the phone until they hang up on you. It probably won't make you feel much better, but as long as you're suffering, why not spread the misery.

Ways to Help Stop Morning Sickness

· ·

1. Avoid getting pregnant.

2. Eat crackers until you feel like a parrot.

3. Don't change your toddler's poopy diapers.

4. Make someone else do the grocery shopping so you don't have to subject yourself to the overpowering smells at the store.

5. Wear those elastic seasickness wristbands. They probably won't help with the morning sickness, but you can bedazzle them so they look like cute bracelets.

6. Eat small amounts frequently.

7. Skip the big-as-your-head, greasy cheeseburger unless you want to see what it looks like partially digested.

8. Take your ~~horse pills~~ prenatal vitamins before going to bed.

9. Suck on hard candies or mints. They won't necessarily keep you from throwing up, but they'll freshen your breath when you do.

10. Skip the health food if it doesn't appeal to you, and stick to the plain ol' rice.

CHAPTER 5

MOVING RIGHT ALONG

(MONTH TWO)

B y the time you hit your second month, you'll start getting used to the idea that you really are pregnant. It still may be quite surreal, but every time you start to think it's just a dream, a bout of nausea will remind you that you are indeed pregnant. Soon you'll start noticing some major changes, if you haven't already. It's amazing how a tiny being the size of a banana slug can make your body change in such huge ways. You'll find yourself hard-pressed to stay awake past 7:00 p.m., and the word *tired* will have a new meaning for you. You may be surprised to find yourself craving strange things. My friend Michelle craved lemons during one of her pregnancies. She craved them so much, she would frequently dream about them. "Oh no, I'm late for school and I forgot my lemons!" She'd awake in a cold sweat, still wanting lemons.

Along with the disagreeable arrival of heartburn and

morning sickness, you'll be pleasantly surprised that your boobs have doubled in size overnight. Actually, you'll probably be too sore and tender to enjoy this little perk.

I'm So Tiredzzzzzzzzzzzzzzzzzz

I'm not talking about ordinary fatigue here. I'm talking about *advanced fatigue.* Okay, I just made that up. But early in your pregnancy, you learn a new meaning for the word *tired.* The tiredness you feel in early pregnancy is like nothing you've ever experienced before. You say you never get tired? You're a go-go-go sort of person. Not anymore. You're used to staying up until 2:00 a.m., you insist? Get ready to hit your pillow, exhausted, by 8:00 p.m. Welcome to pregnancy; you'll sleep through half of it.

I had never experienced the kind of bone-tiredness of pregnancy until I *was* pregnant. I was completely unaware such a state of tiredness even existed, and I was taken by surprise. Seriously, your teeth will be tired. Your hair will be tired. Every cell in your body will be tired. Fighting it is futile.

During my first pregnancy, I didn't work far from my house and most days I drove home to take a nap on my lunch hour. I had twenty to thirty minutes to lie down and rest before I had to drive back to the office. My boss was

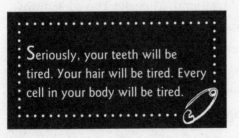

Seriously, your teeth will be tired. Your hair will be tired. Every cell in your body will be tired.

nice enough to let me eat lunch at my desk after I returned so I could take full advantage of my lunch hour
for resting.

If you're able to rest during the day or take a nap, by all
means, do it! If your job doesn't afford you the luxury of
lying down for a few minutes in the middle of the day, you'll
have to plug along without that nap. If you have other little
kids at home, then you had better skip the nap. Unless, of
course, you don't mind taking a chance that the kids won't
burn the house down or paint the dog blue or use scissors
to cut your new slipcovers into doilies. Not that my precious
little angels have ever done anything like that. I've just heard
stories. From other people. About kids who aren't mine.
Ahem.

If you have to skip the nap, then go to bed early. When
your body is telling you it's tired, listen to it. Don't try to
stay up for a show on TV or to finish that book you're reading (unless it's my book *Because I Said So,* in which case, you
should certainly stay up and finish reading it, then leave me
an e-mail about how awesome it is). There will be plenty of
time for that stuff later. Like when your new baby goes off
to college, for example.

Let nonessential things go. You don't have to volunteer
for everything. Let someone else make the two thousand
bake-sale cookies this year. So what if you have dishes piled
to your ceiling. Start teaching your older kids the fine art of
washing pots and pans or just start using paper plates. The
toilet hasn't been cleaned in two months? No problem, just
use your neighbor's bathroom. Learn to let some things go
and rest when you can.

The good thing is that the unbearable fatigue should ease up by the time you hit your fourth month. In the beginning, your body is making your baby's placenta and is adjusting to hormones and huge changes. After three months, when the placenta is functioning on its own and you've adjusted to some of those pregnancy changes, you should have more energy. I know I suddenly felt so much better by my fourth month in each of my pregnancies. Of course, the fatigue all returns with a vengeance after your baby is born and you're up all night with her, but that's another chapter.

Morning Sickness: It Isn't Just for Breakfast Anymore

First off, the term *morning sickness* is a lie. It's a LIE, I tell ya! Nowhere is it written that a pregnant woman who suffers from morning sickness will assuredly find relief by noon. Oh no. It doesn't work that way. Morning sickness can happen in the morning, at lunch, in the afternoon, before dinner, during dinner, after dinner, in the middle of the night, pretty much any time. Granted, for most women who experience morning sickness, it is worse in the morning. After going all night without eating, those women prone to morning sickness will usually feel nauseous upon waking.

That brings me to another point. Not all pregnant women experience morning sickness. In my experience, *you* will be the one to run to the bathroom to empty your stomach and *you* will be the one to feel a little green when you smell dinner cooking. *Your sister* and *your sister-in-law* will not. See how that works? Not everyone will experience morning sickness. To the women who glide through pregnancy without so much as a hint of indigestion, ~~we hope you have a colossally painful delivery~~ how very fortunate for you.

And just how long does morning sickness last? Well, for me and my friends, it lasted about three months. That seems to be the typical amount of time for most women. Generally it eases up when you head into your fourth month. If you're extralucky, it may stick around longer. For your sisters and sisters-in-law, it will probably last one or two hours.

Morning sickness was the absolute bane of my pregnancies. I hate, I mean absolutely *detest* vomiting and avoid it at all costs. I will lie in bed, writhing in pain, willing myself not to get sick all night long before I'd ever get up, head to the bathroom, and just throw up. It NEVER made me feel better. I'm queasy just thinking about it! My friend Jen had morning sickness something fierce. She and her family were at my house one evening when she started feeling nauseous. She said, "If I just throw up, I'm sure I'll feel better." A few minutes later, she excused herself, went to my bathroom, threw up, came out, and said, "I feel much better now. What's for dessert?"

I can't understand this behavior. If that had been me, I would've curled up in a fetal position in the bathroom and sat there crying all night. I sure wouldn't have thrown up and asked what was for dessert immediately afterward! When morning sickness strikes, however, you oftentimes have no choice but to vomit.

So how do you deal with morning sickness? Usually you just have to wait it out for three months. But I have found a few things to help while you're waiting and thinking happy thoughts and trying not to vomit into your purse while at the grocery store. I'll share some of my hard-earned wisdom along with some tips I received from friends, family, doctors, and complete strangers.

1. Eat

Well, duh. I don't know about anyone else, but I pretty much ate anything that wasn't nailed down when I was pregnant. Especially if it included whipped cream.

For me and most of my friends, eating usually helped with our morning sickness. As long as we had something in our stomachs (even just a couple crackers), we felt okay. As soon as our stomachs were empty, the nausea returned. First thing in the morning, I always reached for my handy saltines and ate a couple of them before even getting out of bed and moving around. This didn't always do away with the sickness, but it helped overall. Really, use morning sickness as an excuse to eat whenever you want. Even my sister and sister-in-law, who didn't experience full-blown morning sickness, would get queasy if they hadn't eaten in a while.

This is my number one piece of advice about morning sickness. Don't let yourself get too hungry, or you'll find yourself pulling over to the side of the road on your way to work, so you can dry heave out the window. Learn from my experience. Eat little bits all day for the first three months or so. Oh, and eat whatever sounds and smells good to you. Don't force yourself to eat fish and Brussels sprouts because you think it's healthy. Nobody likes Brussels sprouts anyway. People in Brussels don't even like them. They look like little green brains. And it doesn't do you or your baby any good if it ends up in the toilet before it's been digested. If the only thing that sounds or smells good is cereal or a peanut butter and banana sandwich, then eat that. And keep in mind what foods don't taste too horrible the second time around as they sometimes come back up. My friends and I actually had a whole discussion on which foods were the worst the second time around. I'll spare you the details of that conversation and simply leave you with this: you might want to avoid hamburgers and fries.

2. Sour Candy

Another thing I found to help with the sudden onset of morning sickness was sour candy. Ordinarily I do not like sour candy at all. My kids, on the other hand, love it. Clearly, kids' taste buds are undeveloped, which explains how they can eat Mega Extreme Screaming Sour Candy like it was as mild as a piece of white bread. When I put something like that in my mouth, my face contorts, I grimace, and my lips actually constrict, preventing me from opening my mouth to spit out the offending candy. However, when I was pregnant, there was just something about those sour Altoids or other hard candies that helped soothe my stomach. Maybe it wasn't even the sourness of the candy; perhaps any

> Keep in mind what foods don't taste too horrible the second time around.

candy would've done the trick, but I stuck with the sour ones because they seemed to work for me. Try sucking on a sour hard candy or lollipop and see if that helps to keep your waffles down.

3. Drink Tea with Ginger

Supposedly, ginger has some magical stomach-calming properties. I was told by many people that ginger tea would help settle my tummy. They lied. I tried the whole ginger tea experiment, and it never really did anything for me. I guess I found the warmth of the tea soothing, but let me tell ya, when a whole cup of tea, ginger or otherwise, comes back up on you, it is *not* pleasant.

4. Take Your Prenatal Vitamin at Night

If taking your prenatal vitamin makes you gag or makes you feel more nauseous, try taking it at night before you go to bed. "*If* taking your vitamin makes you feel nauseous." That's pretty funny. Actually, there is no "if." Your prenatal vitamin *will* make you feel nauseous. Know why? Because prenatal vitamins are ~~roughly the size of Utah~~ pretty big. Even if you're a pro at swallowing pills, these will probably cause you to gag a time or two. I was horrible at remembering to take my vitamin in the morning and just naturally took it at night. The times I remembered and took it in the morning, I definitely felt more barfy during the day.

Brushing Your Teeth and Other Triggers

I was supersensitive to anything that came near my mouth. Not only the taste of certain foods made me sick to my stomach, but the textures of some foods made me gag as well. Brushing my teeth always made me gag those first few months. If brushing your teeth makes you gag, well, you're out of luck. You can't go three months without brushing your teeth, so you have to find a way to tolerate it. Maybe switching toothpastes will help. My friend Jen and I decided we just needed to allow ourselves more time to brush so we could brush, gag, brush, gag, brush, throw up, start all over again. . . . There were some days when I just couldn't force myself to brush my teeth at all. That's what gum is for. Shhh, it's our little secret.

The strongest trigger for morning sickness with all six of my pregnancies was odors. Several times, I walked into the grocery store only to turn around and walk right back out. In pregnancy, women tend to have a heightened sense of smell, and all the mingling scents in your typical market can be enough to make you hurl. Changing my toddler's diapers was another thing that made me lose my lunch. If you have an older child in diapers while you're pregnant, I suggest you either

A. Potty-train them immediately (Make sure they know how to wipe and flush, too.)

B. Leave them in their poopy diapers until dad gets home to change them (Of course, this can cause diaper rash of epic proportions and make your whole home stink.)

C. Or, finally, fashion a robot out of household appliances to change your toddler's diapers for you.

Just remember that morning sickness usually lasts only about three months. And then you'll be able to hang it over your child's head when he or she is a teenager and lies to you about completing homework: "I threw up every day when I was pregnant with you and this is the thanks I get?"

Tinkle Tinkle Little Star

With all my pregnancies, I found myself in the bathroom quite a lot. If it wasn't morning sickness that sent me rushing to the bathroom, it was the need to pee. During the first few months, your growing uterus is right next to your bladder, and it can put some considerable pressure on it. For a person used to peeing a couple times a day, these hourly pit stops came as a surprise. During my first pregnancy, back when I used to sleep through the night uninterrupted . . . (Ahhh, I'm having a flashback to those good ole days. I haven't had a full eight hours of uninterrupted sleep in fifteen years. Has it really been that long? Oh, I'm depressed now. Okay, back to peeing . . .) As I was saying, back during my first pregnancy, I had to get up a couple times during the night to go to the bathroom. This was annoying to me. Some people say it's just preparing you for the sleepless nights that lie ahead once Baby arrives. I say, "Forget the preparation! Just let me sleep!" At any rate, early in pregnancy, you'll probably find yourself needing to relieve yourself more frequently than usual. In fact, one time I had to go so badly, I was almost sent to jail. . . .

I was driving home from work one day when I spotted a police officer in my rearview mirror. I did what everyone does in a situation like this. I freaked out. I hadn't blown off any stop signs. I hadn't cut anyone off. I wasn't driving like a maniac or anything. Maybe the officer was following someone else. Uh-oh, there went the lights and siren. I glanced at my speedometer. Oops. There's the problem. I was speeding. I wasn't intentionally breaking the law, but I *was* trying to get home quickly because my eight-month pregnant uterus was pushing on my full bladder, and I was about to have an accident.

I was about two blocks from my house when the police officer flashed the lights. If I stopped and waited for her to write me out a ticket, I would surely pee in my pants. I mean, there was a reason I was speeding in the first place, right? I thought about pulling over, but decided to continue driving to my house. If you've been pregnant, you understand. There's little you can do to control yourself when you've just downed sixteen ounces of apple juice and your baby is kicking your bladder.

I pulled into my driveway like some escaped convict, the police hot on my trail. I jumped out of my car, ran to the police car, which had pulled in behind me, handed the officer my driver's license and explained, "I'm so sorry. I know I was speeding,

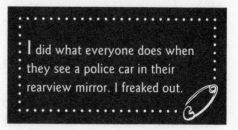

I did what everyone does when they see a police car in their rearview mirror. I freaked out.

but I have to pee so badly! Here's my license, do what you have to do, I'll be right back out."

Without waiting for a reply, I turned on my heel and ran to my front door, disappeared inside, and made a beeline for the bathroom. Ahhh.

After a moment, I returned to the officer, who was standing on my front porch. She eyed my obviously pregnant belly and smiled. She handed my license back to me and said, "I understand. When are you due?"

I told her I was due in four weeks.

"I'm going to let you go this time, but please slow down in the future."

I thanked her profusely and agreed to slow down. I thanked God that this officer believed my true story and didn't think I was running inside my house to hide drugs that were in my car or anything nefarious like that. I could just imagine what could've happened if she'd thought I was up to no good. I'd reemerge from my house to a swat team, rifles trained on me. "But I just had to pee!" I'd whine in defense.

I also thanked God the officer was a woman, presumably a woman who had been pregnant herself at one time. I wonder if that would've worked on a male officer who had never experienced that *I NEED TO GO RIGHT NOW* feeling. I don't think he would have reacted the same way.

Feel the Burn

There's an old wives' tale that says, "If you have a lot of heartburn, you'll have a hairy baby." Well, let me tell ya,

I had so much heart-burn when I was preg-nant with Savannah, I thought I was going to give birth to a chim-panzee. And she did

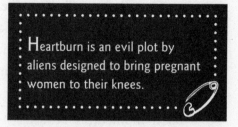

Heartburn is an evil plot by aliens designed to bring pregnant women to their knees.

actually have a lot of hair, come to think of it. Heartburn is ~~an evil plot by aliens designed to bring pregnant women to their knees~~ the result of food coming back up your esopha-gus. As food and stomach acids move along your esophagus, it causes a burning sensation near your heart. I'd never ex-perienced heartburn until I got pregnant for the first time. In fact, I wasn't even sure what it was when I first felt that burning sensation from my stomach, up through my chest to my throat. I thought maybe I was having a heart attack. I was almost ready to call 9-1-1. Thank God I didn't. I can only imagine the doctors rolling their eyes while informing me, "Mrs. Meehan, please stop whining. You're not dying of a heart attack. You just ate one too many ice cream sundaes tonight."

Sometimes I'd awake in the middle of the night with a sudden urge to throw up from the burning feeling of my dinner backing up on me. Like morning sickness, there's not a whole lot you can do to avoid heartburn completely. There are a few tips that can help, though.

1. *Don't eat too late at night.*

Yeah right. I had a hard time following this advice basi-cally because I ate around the clock nonstop. If I didn't eat, I was nauseous. If I did eat, I'd get heartburn. There was no winning for me. But still, if you lie down with a full stomach, there's a good chance that giant ham on rye is going to come right back up on you, sometimes even waking you from sleep. It's a good idea to limit what you eat to just small snacks late in the evening.

2. *Eat small amounts frequently instead of three large meals.*

Now THAT I could do! I had the whole eating-frequently thing down to a science! The good news is that it will help with morning sickness, too. At some point in your pregnancy, you won't even have to make a conscious decision to eat very small amounts at a time. Your uterus will squash your stomach until it's the size of a raisin and that's about all you'll be able to fit in your tummy—a raisin.

3. *Ask your doctor about taking an over-the-counter antacid.*

I personally carried a bottle of Tums with me everywhere I went because I never knew when heartburn would strike. In fact, when I was pregnant with Brooklyn, Clay grabbed the bottle of Tums out of my purse and ate a hefty handful of them. I know, I know, I lost my Mother of the Year trophy for that one. I immediately called Poison Control, who told me, "Don't worry about it. He's just had enough calcium to last a week, and he probably won't get heartburn. Ever." Every time I changed his diaper for the next couple days, it looked like he was pooping chalk. Too graphic? Well, get used to it. Pretty soon you'll be discussing the contents of your baby's diaper over dinner as if it was no different than talking about the weather.

4. *Avoid foods that seem to trigger heartburn in you.*

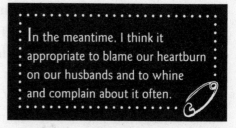

In the meantime. I think it appropriate to blame our heartburn on our husbands and to whine and complain about it often.

If chocolate or coffee or fried foods seem to back up on you, eliminate or at least cut back on them. Ha-ha-ha! Eliminate chocolate! Ha, that's a good one, huh? Okay, here in the real world, we know darn well we aren't going to cut out chocolate. Just be prepared for the ensuing heartburn that will occur after ingesting that most wonderful food of the gods.

Finally, remember that, for most of us, heartburn is a temporary annoyance of pregnancy, and it will go away after we give birth. In the meantime, I think it appropriate to blame it on our husbands and to whine and complain about it often.

The Dolly Parton Syndrome

This is the part of pregnancy that most women (and husbands) don't mind. Right from the beginning, your breasts will get bigger and more tender. Thankfully the tenderness and soreness usually go away after the first two or three months, and you'll be left with movie-star breasts that both you and your husband will love. Unless, of course, you happen to be like me and had plenty enough to begin with. For us, instead of having fun new playthings that look like cantaloupes, we're blessed with breasts that more closely resemble basketballs. I had to search high and low for an industrial-strength bra the size of Texas, with fifteen hooks down the back and underwire made of steel I beams to support them.

And support is important. Wear a good, supportive bra. In fact, you might even want to go to a nice department store that offers fittings to make sure you're getting the right size. Buy only one or two, though, because your breasts will continue to grow throughout your pregnancy, and the bra you buy today probably won't fit next month.

If you've never been especially endowed in the breast department, enjoy it while it lasts, because unfortunately, like all things good, it will eventually come to an end. Those babies will deflate just as soon as you're done nursing your little one or sooner if you choose not to breastfeed. If you were large to begin with, well, let's not talk about what will happen when the air is let out of those basketballs. I don't want to scare anyone with tales of how you'll have to either roll up your boobs and stuff them into your bra or tuck them into the waistband of your pants. Nope, we won't talk about that here.

I Just Have a Taste for a Cheeseburger Topped with Caramel Sauce and Calamari

In old black-and-white movies, you always see the pregnant woman send her husband out in the middle of the night for pickles and ice cream. Now I don't personally know anyone who has eaten that combination (except my teenage son, but he's not pregnant, just weird), though I have had some strong cravings and aversions myself while pregnant. I never had uncontrollable hankerings for sweet-and-sour chicken tempura topped with chocolate sauce or deep-fried zucchini over cherry ice cream, but I did crave ice cream. This is why I lived at Dairy Queen when I was pregnant with my first child. Even though I don't ordinarily love ice cream, I just couldn't get enough of it while I was carrying my son. Yep, I sure craved ice cream. And Swedish fish. And watermelon. And cherry slushies. Oh yeah, and pizza. And hot dogs. And grapes. And tiramisu. And, well, okay I basically craved everything. They say that what you eat while pregnant could affect your offspring's tastes. Maybe that would explain why my oldest son just asked for beef jerky and M&M's for dinner.

On the flipside, I developed an absolute aversion to Mexican food. Up until I was pregnant, I had loved Mexican food, so it was unusual for me to turn up my nose at it, but when I was nine weeks pregnant with my first child, Austin, I got food poisoning after eating a burrito as big as my head. I ended up in the hospital and thought I was going to die. While in the hospital, I got to have my first ultrasound of my baby because the doctors wanted to make sure everything was okay with him. When they handed me the ultrasound picture of my baby, I remember thinking they'd surely made a mistake and had inadvertently given me a picture of a June bug instead because, in my mind, there was *no way* that little buglike thing was a baby. Anyway, Austin was fine and after a couple days I was fine, too. But I didn't eat Mexican food again for a good eight years after that.

All my friends experienced cravings of some sort during their pregnancies. If you're constantly cravings foods that aren't so good for you, you might need to ~~hide in the closet to eat them~~ try to find an acceptable substitute to ensure your baby is getting the nutrition he needs and you're not packing on more pounds than you need. Otherwise, go ahead and give in; satisfy your craving. And if workers at the fast-food joint look at you strangely when you ask for extra caramel sauce on that cheeseburger, just tell them it's for your teenage son.

Stupid Things People Say to Pregnant Women

. . . .

1. *When are you due?* Unless you actually see Baby's head crowning, never ask a woman this!

2. *Should you be doing that in your condition?* Unless the mother-to-be is chugging whiskey and smoking while riding a mechanical bull, it's best that you butt out and not question how she's taking care of her unborn child.

3. *You should be doing [fill in the blank].* Much like the previous tip, it's best if you mind your own business.

The following questions are generally directed at parents who already have a couple children.

1. *You're pregnant again? Don't you know what causes that?* Of course we know what causes it, don't you???

2. *Aren't you done yet?* I figure we'll keep going until we get an ugly one.

3. *Are you trying to overpopulate the earth?* No, we're just trying to outnumber the idiots.

CHAPTER 6

ALMOST DONE THROWING UP

(MONTH THREE)

During the third month of all my pregnancies, I started to feel fat and unattractive. I was beginning to gain a little weight, yet I didn't look pregnant. My jeans were starting to get tight, yet maternity clothes were huge on me. I was tired all the time and most days couldn't find the energy to comb my hair. I was also tired of feeling nauseous and having to run to the bathroom every time I smelled something strong. The initial excitement and novelty was wearing off, and I wondered how I'd ever make it through another six months of this. In addition to all the symptoms I'd already developed, new ones popped up to add to my discomfort.

Woosh Woosh Woosh Woosh

But it wasn't all pain and misery. A really cool thing happens during the third month: you get to hear Baby's heartbeat for the first time. This never got old with any of my pregnancies. Every single time I heard that heartbeat for the first time, I got emotional and teared up. That heartbeat is the most amazing sound you'll hear when you're pregnant. Unless, of course, you're lucky enough to hear things like your husband telling you, "You look so wonderful! You were much too skinny before. You just look so awesome pregnant." Or maybe, "Let me get that for you. You just lie down and I'll rub your feet and get you a sparkling water. Can I do anything else for you, dear?" One can dream, right?

Before they have an ultrasound exam, most women will hear their baby's heartbeat at a routine appointment when their doctor uses a stethoscope or Doppler to pick up the fetal heart tones. Your physician will probably use a Doppler, which, although it sounds like something your local weatherman might use, is just a little device for measuring your baby's heart tones. I'm sure there's a very technical explanation of how this works, but alas, I'm no mathematician or scientist. The very nontechnical explanation is this: your doctor will move a small piece of plastic over your abdomen and when it picks up your baby's heartbeat, you'll hear a kind of *woosh woosh woosh* sound. Your baby's heart doesn't actually make a woosh sound—it beats just like yours or mine—but the sound you'll hear is a wooshy kind of sound because of some scientific reason. It's a most wonderful, comforting sound and one you'll never forget.

Your physician may be able to pick up your baby's heartbeat as early as twelve weeks, but don't freak out if it isn't detectable then.

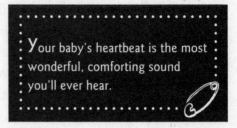

Your baby's heartbeat is the most wonderful, comforting sound you'll ever hear.

Actually, scratch that last part. There's no telling a pregnant woman not to freak out when it comes to her baby. There's honestly no reason to freak out, but being pregnant and anxious, I know darn well that you'll freak out if you don't hear your baby's heartbeat by twelve weeks. I know this because I freaked out when I was pregnant with Jackson and my doctor couldn't detect a heartbeat. I lay there, just waiting to hear the horrible news that my baby wasn't thriving. Yep, I freaked out. We women freak out over all sorts of things while we're pregnant, and it only gets worse after our babies are born.

But back to the heartbeat. There really isn't a reason to be anxious if you don't hear your baby's heartbeat at twelve weeks. Twelve weeks is on the early side of when you'll be able to hear it. Different factors can affect when you're able to hear the heartbeat. Maybe the baby is lying in a weird way and the heartbeat just can't be picked up by this instrument. Or perhaps you've already had five kids and you have a little extra, um, *fluff* around your middle. This can hinder your doctor's ability to pick up Baby's heart tones. Certainly by twenty weeks, you should be able to hear your baby's heart tones with a Doppler. If your doctor still can't pick up the heartbeat at this time, he'll probably order an ultrasound to double-check on Baby's well-being.

When I was pregnant with my fifth baby, Clayton, I took my older kids to my doctor's appointment to hear the baby's heartbeat. The older ones sat in the office sulking and saying things like, "We're bored," and "Why did we have to come here?" and "How much longer will it be?" The younger kids dumped every toy they owned out of a backpack onto the floor of the exam room and whined that they were hungry. The doctor finally walked in and soon picked up Baby's heartbeat with the Doppler. When that sweet *woosh woosh woosh woosh* started, I teared up. I smiled at my kids knowing that the wonderful sound meant my baby was alive and well, growing inside me. I expected them to smile back at me and express some lovely sentiment. Instead, they looked at me and said things like, "That's it? You dragged us here for *that*? That doesn't even sound like a heartbeat!" Enjoy the moments of listening to your baby's heartbeat, because all too soon it will be replaced by other sounds, such as complaining and whining.

Is That a Road Map on Your Legs?

Another fun thing that happens to many women during pregnancy is the occurrence of varicose veins. I was one of those unfortunate souls who developed varicose veins during my first pregnancy, and they got worse throughout each subsequent pregnancy. By the time I was pregnant with Brooklyn, my left leg looked like a road map of Cincinnati with all the blueish purple ropey veins crisscrossing my calf.

Varicose veins run in families, which means you should get on the phone and start yelling at your mom and grandmother for passing on lousy genes to you.

Varicose veins often rear their ugly head for the first time during pregnancy. The same hormonal changes that make you want to throw things at your husband when he says something stupid are also partly to blame for your venous problems. Besides the hormones, there's increased blood volume for your veins to handle and increased pressure from your growing uterus, which puts more pressure on your veins.

Some women who develop varicose veins in pregnancy may only have mildly achy legs. With my first pregnancy, that was my only symptom. My veins showed through my skin and were slightly bumpy and achy. I was pregnant throughout the summer but refused to wear shorts when the ugly veins started showing, because I was embarrassed by them. That didn't last too long, however. Because your thermostat gets turned way up when you're pregnant, the overwhelming heat won out over the ugly veins in the end. I took a chance on people gaping at my veiny legs. I needn't have worried, however. People were much too busy staring at my enormous belly to notice my legs. With each subsequent pregnancy, however, they got worse. You might experience mild pain, icky-looking veins, or all-out pain and discomfort with raised, bumpy, itchy skin over the veins.

You should get on the phone and start yelling at your mom and grandmother for passing on lousy genes to you.

A blood clot is a rare complication that can occur in pregnant women, especially those with varicose veins. Women who smoke, have a blood-clotting disorder, are over age thirty or overweight, have had three or more deliveries, or have been on bed rest may be at an increased risk for developing clots.

If you suspect any kind of blood clot or if you have pain in your legs, especially upon flexing your feet, seek medical attention. Blood clots are nothing to mess around with. I know, not because I'm a doctor, but because I developed blood clots during my sixth pregnancy. I waddled into the emergency room, told the nurse that I was pregnant, showed her my red, swollen leg, complained of terrible pain, and was immediately whisked back and seen by a doctor. (Really, the next time you're in the waiting room at your local ER, just tell them you're pregnant and you think you have a blood clot, even if you're only there because you have the sniffles. You'll have a much shorter wait!) I had to spend a few days in the hospital where I had an elderly roommate who was getting ready for a colonoscopy. She had to um, empty, her, um, digestive system every few minutes at a bedside commode. Let me tell ya, it was not fun being in the same room, considering I had a whopping case of morning sickness at the time. Oops, I got off track there. Thankfully, my clots were managed with injected blood thinners that I had to continue using throughout my pregnancy, and highly sexy medical-grade compression stockings.

There are a couple things you can do to help prevent varicose veins, but sometimes they're just unavoidable.

* *Don't gain too much weight.* Ha-ha-ha-ha, I crack myself up. No, seriously, try not to gain too much weight. The more weight you gain, the more pressure on those poor leg veins.
* *Don't smoke.* You shouldn't be doing this anyway.
* *Change position frequently.* Don't sit or stand for long periods without taking a break and moving around. Especially if you travel. If you're traveling by car, make frequent stops, get out and stretch your legs. If you're traveling by plane, get up and walk up and down the aisles a couple times during your flight. While seated, move your feet around, flex your toes, and kick the seat in front of you. Other passengers love this.
* *Don't lift heavy stuff.* That's what your husband or dad or muscular male friends are for.
* *Get a little exercise every day.* I suggest walking to the refrigerator, tying your shoes, and getting out of bed. Experts recommend a twenty-minute walk. Take your pick.

As with everything in pregnancy, listen to your body and seek medical attention if you ever have any questions, unusual symptoms, or if something doesn't seem right. And by all means, don't take medical advice from a crazy woman with no medical training and six kids draining her brain cells. Well, except for the advice about consulting a medical professional if you have any questions. You can take that advice from me.

You Just "Glow"

You've heard that saying, right? How a pregnant woman just "glows"? Well, I'll let you in on a little secret. That magical *glow* is really just oily skin. Yep, that's right. We don't glow; we just have the skin of a teenager. You may even find yourself breaking out for the first time in years. About the only thing you can do, other than wearing a burka until you give birth, is to wash your face ~~fifty~~ a couple times a day and keep in mind that this condition will eventually pass.

When You Just Can't "Go"

Another fun (and by *fun,* I mean "rotten") thing that happens to many women during pregnancy is constipation. It's just another way our bodies show us they've been taken over by aliens. Yes, I know, it doesn't seem right to speak about such an amazing thing as pregnancy in terms of aliens, but if you've ever been pregnant, you know what I mean. Yes, pregnancy is an absolute miracle. Yes, pregnancy is a magical, wondrous time. But pregnancy is also a time when it just feels like your body is no longer your own. All these strange things are happening, and you have no control over them.

Constipation is just one more of those things.

You want to deal with constipation right away, not only because it's uncomfortable, but

> Constipation is just another way our bodies show us they've been taken over by aliens.

because if you don't, you could end up with a bonus problem—hemorrhoids! They tend to go hand in hand with constipation. Doctors say the best way to deal with constipation is to avoid it altogether if possible. Yeah right. You know how you do that? You avoid getting pregnant.

For those of us who are already pregnant and have no way to avoid it, you can help keep your bowels from backing up on you by drinking plenty of fluids—water and juice. If you're really having problems with constipation, you might even try gagging down some prune juice. Hey, when you're that uncomfortable, you'll be willing to do crazy things—even drinking prune juice.

If it's really bad, you may have to forgo the chocolate and ice cream (the horror!) and make sure you're getting enough fiber in your diet instead. I know, I know, it's a toss-up. Constipation versus eating plenty of fresh fruit and veggies, whole grains, and legumes. Constipation, eating fiber. Constipation, eating fiber. It's your call. But if you're not used to eating a diet high in fiber, you might want to add fiber slowly or you may find yourself with stomach cramps, flatulence, and/or diarrhea, which is not really an improvement to constipation. Hey, no one said pregnancy was glamorous.

Are You Pregnant or Have You Just Gained a Few Pounds?

I think the thing I disliked the most about this point in pregnancy is the fact that I didn't look pregnant. I didn't look good. I didn't look like myself. But I didn't look pregnant, either. I remember just waiting for my belly to get bigger so my pregnancy would be obvious. My friend Denise said it would be nice to have a T-shirt that read "I'm not fat, I'm pregnant." That's pretty much how all my friends felt at this point. You're gaining weight, your middle is expanding, yet you don't look obviously pregnant yet. That in-between stage just stinks.

Finding clothes to fit properly was quite a feat, too. You're starting to outgrow your jeans, yet when you try on a pair of maternity pants, they're so big, they fall off. I have a great secret for getting a little more use out of your jeans before you move into maternity clothes. It's called the rubber band trick. What you do is loop a sturdy rubber band through the button hole closure in the top of your jeans. Then you hook the other end of the rubber band over the button. This way, you can still wear your jeans even though they're too tight to button. Just make sure you wear a long shirt to cover your rubber-banded–together pants. This usu-ally bought me an extra month or so, and by the time I could no longer use the rubber band trick, I was able to fit into maternity pants. Just don't push it and use the rubber band trick too long. When your belly gets too big for your pants, even with the rubber band, it's time to move into ma-ternity clothes. Once I made the mistake of trying to use the rubber band for a little too long. It really hurts when the rubber band snaps and slaps you in the stomach.

This is the time the gossip and whispers start. "Is she pregnant or isn't she?" My friend Stacie, who also has six kids, was certain her coworkers had an office pool about whether she was pregnant yet again when she started showing with her sixth baby. She could just hear them whispering, "Well it *has* been two years since her last . . ."

To alleviate other people's confusion—Is she just getting fat, or is she pregnant?—you can arch your back and stick your tummy out as far as you can. Rest your hands on your abdomen at all times and say things like, "Oh, this baby is really giving me heartburn today!" and "Oh, I just can't decide on a name for this baby!" as loudly as you can to all within earshot. Yes, it will certainly make your back hurt to stand like that, but it's better than having complete strangers think you're fat.

Crazy Things Pregnant Women Do Because of "Baby Brain"

1. Put their car keys in the refrigerator

2. Cry when Hallmark commercials come on TV

3. Wear two different-colored shoes to work

4. Forget their husband's name

5. Lose their purse, keys, coat, shoes

6. Throw large objects at their husbands when they suggest that they're acting irrationally

7. Get unnaturally excited over the diaper bag selection at Babies "R" Us

8. Won't be able to concentrate on anything but picking out a baby name for weeks on end

9. Tell complete strangers in line at the grocery store all the details of their heartburn, nausea, or constipation problems

10. Decide they need a radical new hairstyle, pronto

CHAPTER 7

ENTERING THE SECOND TRIMESTER!

(MONTH FOUR)

T his is my favorite time in pregnancy. Usually in the fourth month, all the yucky symptoms disappear. One morning you wake up and realize you don't need to throw up. Hallelujah, the morning sickness is gone! You don't spend every minute of every day nauseated anymore. You no longer have to run to the bathroom every few minutes to pee, either. As your uterus rises, it doesn't squish your bladder as much, so you no longer need to know where the nearest bathroom is wherever you go.

In the fourth month, you finally start looking pregnant. By the ninth month, you'll be plenty tired of looking pregnant, but trust me, it'll be exciting when your belly starts sticking out, announcing to the world that you have a new life growing inside you. I loved being able to break out the maternity clothes and actually have them fit. Of course, with my second baby, maternity clothes were just *my clothes.*

By the time you hit your fourth month, the horrible, debilitating fatigue disappears. Suddenly, one day, you'll find you can stay awake in the evening. Most women have energy and feel like a million bucks. This is the time to get baby's room ready—while you're feeling good, you have energy, and the moodiness, nausea, and breast tenderness of the early months is gone. And before you enter your third trimester, when you feel like a beached whale and you're too sore to move.

The most wonderful thing that happens around this time is that you'll begin to feel your baby move. There really aren't words to describe how utterly awesome this feeling is. It's just another confirmation that your baby is alive and doing well. At this point, there should be no doubt about your pregnancy. The reality of it has certainly hit home. Unless, of course, you're like my friend Denise, who had a bad case of denial and just didn't believe she was pregnant until she actually gave birth.

Although my friends and I all agree that this was the best time in our pregnancies, it's not without any symptoms or discomforts. You'll find yourself losing your mind soon if you haven't already. Headaches and insomnia often come into play as well.

Still, enjoy this time. I'm not saying that it gets worse later on. I don't want to scare anyone, but just trust me on this. Enjoy it now.

Baby Brain

I'm not talking about the development of your baby's brain here. Nope, in this case, the term *baby brain* refers to a state of mind, or lack thereof. This is something that happens to all pregnant women. It cannot be avoided. It's futile to try. Most pregnant women first notice symptoms of baby brain early in their pregnancy. Perhaps, while watching TV, you see a commercial for IHOP and decide you simply must have pancakes. Now. You walk into the kitchen to whip up a batch of fluffy buttermilk pancakes to satisfy your craving. Upon arrival in the kitchen, however, you completely forget your purpose for walking in. Repeat after me, "I know I came in here for a reason!" You'll be saying this a lot during your pregnancy. Welcome to baby brain!

Suddenly you'll find things just flying out of your brain. You will no longer have enough memory space for trivial things like your Social Security number, your husband's name, and the fact that you were supposed to pick up your son from baseball practice at seven. This is because your baby sucks the brain cells right out of your head. I truly couldn't seem to remember anything when I was pregnant. I think this is when I started making lists. I'd spend an hour making out a grocery list, knowing that if I didn't, I'd forget essentials like milk, bread, and chocolate while shopping. Of course, more often than not, I'd forget to bring the list when I left for the store. I guess that kinda defeated the whole purpose of the list.

You will lose not only your mind but objects as well. My friend Melissa was especially bad at losing things while she was pregnant with her second daughter. I think I received an e-mail from her every week asking, "If you were a set of car keys, where would you be?" Or "So, do you have any ideas where I might have put my purse this time?" One time she left her cell phone in the cart while shopping at The Home Depot and another time she lost her day planner in her car. Your memory just won't work as well as it used to while you're pregnant.

One day, while running late for a doctor's appointment, I couldn't find my car keys. I looked high and low for them. After several minutes, I gave up, called my friend, and begged her to drive me to the doctor. As I opened my fridge to grab my pee cup, I found my keys sitting next to it. In the fridge. Now, this may sound crazy to you if you've never been pregnant, but I guarantee that the women who have been pregnant before are reading this and nodding their heads in agreement. Keys in the fridge, shoes in your lingerie drawer, driver's license next to your toothpaste—all perfectly normal in the land of pregnancy.

I remember going to the mall with my kids while I was pregnant with my fifth baby, Clayton. After shopping for a couple hours, we walked out to the parking lot and headed for my van. As we reached the vehicle, I opened the passenger door and threw my bags on the seat. My kids all stood at my side just staring at me. "Why are you standing there? Get in the car! Let's go!" I said impatiently.

Austin finally spoke up and said, "Um, Mom? This isn't our car."

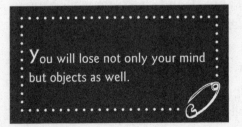

You will lose not only your mind but objects as well.

"What do you mean it's not our car? Of course it is! Get in right now please before . . ." I trailed off as I noticed a pack of cigarettes and a couple toys that didn't belong to us on the seat. Oh my gosh! My kids were right! This wasn't our car! I quickly grabbed my bags off the front seat and speedily backed away from the van, all the while praying that the actual owners wouldn't walk out at that moment. Or, worse yet, that Security wouldn't come up and accuse me of stealing the bags out of someone else's car. My kids will never let me live that one down and still, to this day, whenever we're in a parking lot, they ask me in a very smart-aleck fashion, "Are you sure this is our car, Mom?"

I think the term *baby brain* could really be used to describe a wide variety of strange happenings—not just your lack of memory. For example, pregnant women do *a lot* of daydreaming. They dream about their babies. They dream about childbirth. They dream about watching their sons win the Little League series. They dream about their daughters going to prom.

They also dream when they're asleep. The most vivid dreams I've ever had in my life were while I was pregnant. Those dreams always seemed so real, too! Oftentimes, while we were pregnant, my friends and I would ask each other the same question: What do you suppose this dream means? Yes, we had the usual assortment of dreams, like forgetting the baby after we left the hospital or not knowing what to do with the baby once we got home. We had dreams that we couldn't remember the baby's name or that every store in the state ran out of diapers. I had a dream once where a clown was riding on a motorcycle and then the clown

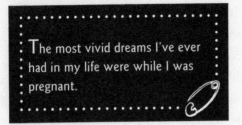

The most vivid dreams I've ever had in my life were while I was pregnant.

turned into Oprah, and she took me for a ride to Paris. But when we got there, it wasn't really Paris but rather the hospital, and then I gave birth to twelve babies, and I was so upset because I really wanted more. Then I named them all Bob, even the girls, and my doctor, who was my ninth-grade typing teacher, told me that I had to sing and dance onstage before I could take my babies, who were now five years old, home. Anyway, my point is, weird dreams come with the territory when you're pregnant.

Another baby brain symptom is that your view of reality may be a bit distorted—in an overly positive way. You will probably, at some point, look at things through a pair of heavily frosted, rose-colored glasses. You may glance at your children and see only a couple of beautiful angels who can do no wrong despite the fact that they're pummeling each other with pillows as you look on. Oftentimes a pregnant woman's vision is, shall we say, *clouded.* This is the same ailment responsible for those times you drive home from work, arrive at your house, and don't remember how you got there. And just as your point of view can be distorted so you see everything in a positive light, it can change on a dime and be distorted so you see everything as Oscar the Grouch would. Suddenly your husband, who was nice enough to make a smoothie for a snack after dinner, is a horrible, uncaring man because he used bananas, *BANANAS,* in the smoothie, and as of this morning, you have decided you hate bananas. How could he not know this? A caring husband would know this! And you'll cry, "No one loves me!" You'll probably do a lot of this crazy, irrational crying during your pregnancy. Still, the irrational crying is probably better than threatening the father of your child with, "If you don't learn to chew more quietly, I'll kill you, and I watch enough *CSI* that I could do it and make it look like an accident, too!"

For example, in the movie *Look Who's Talking*, Kirstie Alley starts sobbing uncontrollably when a commercial for fabric softener comes on TV. This is not just some crazy concept they came up with for television. Oh no. It happens, my friends. In fact, it happens more often than you might think. I think every pregnant woman has at least a couple of these emotional outbursts during her pregnancy. I remember tearing up often during worship service. Now, my pastor can give a wonderful, moving sermon, but alas, that wasn't the reason I would tear up. He could simply be saying, "Please be seated," and I'd be so overcome with emotion, I'd have to immediately find some tissue.

My point is . . . wait, what was my point? I know I had a point here. What was I going to say? Grrr, I'm sure it'll come to me eventually. . . .

You Know What You Need to Do . . .

As your pregnancy becomes more apparent, strangers come out of the woodwork to give you advice you never knew you needed. Kind, grandmotherly women are especially good for this. They grew up in a time where it took a village to raise children. It was being neighborly to tell a poor, unknowing pregnant woman what she should be doing. It was their *duty* to pass down their hard-earned knowledge to the next generation. Or two. Or three.

When I had my first baby, I was told repeatedly to lay him down on his tummy so he wouldn't aspirate anything if he spit up. By my second baby, things had changed and I was told to lay her on her side with receiving blankets rolled up and wedged alongside her so she wouldn't roll over. Things changed again by the time I had my third baby and there was a huge Back to Sleep campaign where all new mothers were told to lay their babies on their backs to help prevent the possibility of SIDS. Moms today are probably being told to have their babies sleep standing up. My point is just that as research is done and new discoveries are made, advice and attitudes change. And although Grandma means well, things just aren't the same as they were when she had your mother.

Strangers feel this overwhelming need to tell pregnant women what they're doing wrong and how they should be doing it. If you reach for some files off a high shelf at work, in will swoop someone who will inform you that reaching like that can wrap the umbilical cord around Baby's neck. People will make comments on what you eat: "Do you really think you

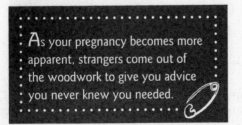

As your pregnancy becomes more apparent, strangers come out of the woodwork to give you advice you never knew you needed.

should be eating those chili dogs in your condition?" They'll give advice on pain relief: "Oh you don't want to take any drugs in childbirth. They're bad for the baby." Or, "Oh you must get an epidural the minute you arrive at the hospital or you'll keel over in pain." They'll give you advice on exercise, hospital choice, doctor choice, what you should or shouldn't be lifting, working on, cleaning. Although it is usually well intentioned, this unsolicited advice can be annoying.

The good thing is, you can smile, nod your head, and then promptly ignore everything they've said because you'll never see them again. When I was pregnant and people felt the need to put their two cents in, I just said, "Okay," and promptly forgot what they said. It really didn't bother me much. I figured they (for the most part) were just trying to be helpful even if most of the advice I received was silly. I wasn't one to get bent out of shape over it. If, however, you get highly irritated by unwanted advice, you might want to have a response ready ahead of time for when you're accosted by a well-meaning, misinformed stranger. Something along the lines of, "You can't tell me what to do." works. You can also try plugging your ears and chanting, "La la la la la la la, I'm not listening!" Or I suppose you could be nice and just tell them, "Thank you, I'll bring that up to my doctor."

But it's not the same when it's your mother, grandmother, mother-in-law, aunt, or older sister who gives you this advice. You'll probably have to see and talk to these people again at some point in your life, so it's a good idea to learn how to deal with unsolicited advice in a nice way.

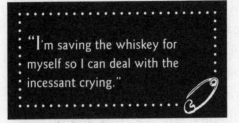

"I'm saving the whiskey for myself so I can deal with the incessant crying."

For example, when your grandmother tells you that she never used a car seat in her life and her kids all lived, you could respond with, "Are you kidding? I've seen the way you drive!" Or, you could say, "Times have changed, Grandma, and it's quite illegal to drive your kids without using car seats. You wouldn't want to see your favorite granddaughter wind up in jail now, would you?"

Your mom might insist that babies should be fed cereal from the time they're one week old, or that babies should be placed on their tummies to sleep. You could tell her that she clearly has no clue how to parent. Mothers don't generally take kindly to being told they're horrible parents, though, and if you choose that route, you should expect your mother to take you on a fun-filled guilt trip that will last at least a year. My sister and I like to joke around, instead. "So, Mom, how many older brothers and sisters did we have before you laid them on their tummies to sleep?"

When my first child was teething, my mother-in-law told me to rub some whiskey on my baby's gums to soothe him. I told her, "Actually, I'm saving the whiskey for myself so I can deal with the incessant crying." And then I made a mental note to never let my mother-in-law babysit my child.

Here's the really scary part—you're bound to turn into your mother and start giving unsolicited advice one day. I'm telling you, it happens! My sister was pregnant with her second baby when we were at a family party. There were sandwiches on a table, and my sister was hungry, but she refused to eat.

"Why don't you have a sandwich?" I asked.

She looked at me like I was daft and said, "Because I'm pregnant (duh!)."

"I don't get it. Have a sandwich."

"I can't eat lunch meat!" She said the words "lunch meat" the same way one might say "rat poison" or "arsenic" or "liver." I stared at her, clueless as to what lunch meat had to do with anything. She explained that pregnant women were not supposed to eat lunch meat. That was a new one to me. I, of course, was totally understanding and supportive as I told her, "That's the most ridiculous thing I've ever heard. I ate lunch meat throughout my pregnancies and my kids turned out perfectly normal!" Right on cue, my son Clay passed us, wearing his pants on his arms, his shirt on his legs, and walking backward. My sister cast a dubious look between me and my son.

One topic that everyone loves to give advice on is baby names. My sister was so dead set against hearing any advice on baby names that she refused to tell anyone the names she was considering for her soon-to-be baby until well after he was born. And maybe she was wise to do that, since it seems like everyone has an opinion when it comes to the age-old question "What do we name the baby?" My son Clayton really wanted my sister to name her baby Lightning McQueen. My brother-in-law, Sam, the 493rd, really wanted their baby to be named Sam, the 494th. My sister thought it might be just a tad bit confusing with so many "Sams" in the family and was adamant about not having a "junior."

I personally didn't care what she named her child, I just wanted to hear the names she was considering so I could put it my two cents!

If you're pregnant, you are guaranteed to get advice on naming your child. You should name him after your great-great-grandfather. I think you should give her a unique name. Oh, you have to name him after me! You must name her after your great grandmother Mary Angela Theresa Celeste, God rest her soul. I think you should give him a Greek name to pay tribute to our heritage. Jackson insisted we name Clay either Nemo or Slicker. We decided to go with Clayton, but Jackson called him Slicker for a good year.

My kids are all named after cities. It didn't start that way, but after the first two, I realized I had a theme going and I needed to stick with it. By the time I was pregnant with my fifth and sixth babies, I had a hard time coming up with names I liked. Fortunately for me, I had friends, family, and strangers who were more than willing to give me helpful suggestions like Tallahassee, Punxsutawney, Schenectady, and Rancho Cucamonga. I'm pretty sure you're guaranteeing your child will be beaten up daily at school if you name him Schenectady. Not to mention the fact that he probably wouldn't learn how to spell his name until well into the third grade.

There is no way to avoid this advice. Even if you do like my sister and refuse to discuss name possibilities until your baby is born, people will ask about it every time they talk to you, and you'll be forced to explain your position time and time again. And really, you don't avoid the advice by doing it this way; you simply *delay* it. After my nephew was born and my sister announced his name, Samuel Dominick, she

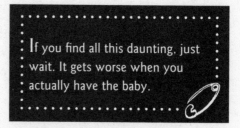

If you find all this daunting. just wait. It gets worse when you actually have the baby.

still had to field questions and comments and advice.

"Oh so you *did* agree to name him Samuel the 494th." "Oh, you're only putting Samuel on paper, but you're calling him Dominick?" "Then why didn't you just name him Dominick?" "You know, I've never seen Dominick spelled with a *k* before. It looks like the grocery store name, Dominick's." "I think he looks more like an Alex." "I still think you should've named him Benjamin."

Naming your baby is just one of the many things that family members, friends, coworkers, and complete strangers will want to get in on. There's no way to avoid it. About all you can do is grin and bear it and record some of the more ridiculous advice in your child's baby book so you can share a good laugh later. If you find all this daunting, just wait. It gets worse when you actually have the baby.

Indigestion, Gas Bubble, or (Gasp!) Baby?

Feeling my baby move was by far the ~~only good part~~ best part of pregnancy for me. There's just something about feeling that little baby squirming around inside you that makes it all real. Up until you feel those first movements, you just have to trust your doctor that you are indeed pregnant and there's really a new life growing inside you. Once you start feeling her move, you *know* you're pregnant. Those first little flutters are almost magical. I remember lying awake at night, holding perfectly still, just concentrating, waiting to feel another little confirmation of the life inside my abdomen.

It's fun guessing if those first little twitches are actually Baby's movements or just indigestion. It's hard to tell the difference at first. Especially when it's your first baby and you're not sure what to expect. It can take a few times before you realize that those fluttery feelings are actually caused by your baby.

Some of my friends thought something was brushing against their abdomen on the outside, but when they looked down, they realized nothing was touching them. It was their baby moving. Other friends have described those first movements as feeling like gas bubbles. One friend kept trying to burp to alleviate the gassy feeling before she realized it was her baby that she was feeling.

First-time moms can usually feel those first movments sometime between eighteen and twenty-four weeks. Mothers who have given birth before know what it feels like and generally will recognize those first flutters a little sooner. Plus, the uterus—along with everything else in a mom who has already given birth—is a little more stretched out, making it easier to feel Baby's movements.

Of course, those magical first little flutters are eventually replaced with full-blown kicks to the bladder causing you to pee in your pants, and little feet wedged up in your rib cage causing awful pain. When I was pregnant with Jackson, he kicked a lot. I was convinced he was going to be crowned the Ultimate Fighting Champion before he was even born. If you feel little rhythmic movements that come at frequent, fairly regular intervals, your baby probably has the hiccups! It's fun to feel your baby jump with each hiccup; they usually last for several minutes.

When Baby gets bigger and really starts squirming around, kicking and moving, you can actually see the movements through your belly. It's amazing how much time a pregnant woman can spend just watching her abdomen move. I remember watching my abdomen rise and fall with my baby's movements. I was in awe. This life inside me is moving and it's just so real. And so sweet. And so amazing. And so much like the movie *Alien*.

Every pregnant woman knows that babies like to play tricks on moms. Your baby can be kicking for twenty minutes straight, but the minute you try to get your husband or mom or sister or friend to put their hand on your belly so they can feel her move, she'll stop. Without fail. Every time. The minute your husband or mom or sister or friend gives up and walks away, the baby will start moving again because the baby is laughing so hard at you. This is a fun game they like to play.

These first fluttery movements are my favorite part of pregnancy. Enjoy them!

Counting Sheep

Some women experience insomnia during pregnancy. And by *some*, I actually mean ALL pregnant women. Whoever coined the phrase "sleeping like a baby" clearly doesn't have a baby. Babies don't sleep through the night and neither do pregnant women. I haven't had a full night's sleep in sixteen years!

The minute you see that positive pregnancy test, you can pretty much give up on a good night's sleep for the rest of your life. You'll wake up to pee several times a night. You'll wake up because you're suffering from heartburn. You'll lie awake because your hips hurt or your hands are numb. Despite your extreme fatigue, there will be nights when you just can't sleep.

While you're lying awake at night, try changing positions to get comfortable. Make loud sighing noises and use great effort in flopping back and forth as you try to find a comfy position that will allow you to sleep. It won't help you fall asleep any faster, but it will ensure that your husband won't be able to sleep, either. Why should you be the only one to suffer, right? Or I suppose you could be nice and just hoist yourself out of bed and do something useful like folding laundry, paying bills, reading a book of baby names, arranging the bedding in Baby's crib for the four thousandth time, or watching old Seinfeld reruns.

It won't just be physical discomforts that keep you up at night. You'll also lie awake wondering about your baby. What will he look like? Will she be a talented artist like her aunt? Will he be good at sports? I hope she's born with ten fingers and ten

> Some women experience insomnia during pregnancy. And by *some*, I mean ALL.

toes. I pray I can teach him well and that he grows up to be a productive member of society. Most important, I hope he doesn't have Uncle Max's nose! You'll probably spend a lot of time daydreaming and worrying about your little one. If you think you're losing sleep worrying about them now, just wait until they're actually born. And if you think you spend a lot of time worrying about your newborn, just wait until he starts driving!

Looking Stylish!

Maternity clothes are pretty darn stylish today. They look just about like any regular clothes for sale out there. Back when I was pregnant with my first couple kids, pants only came with the huge stretchy belly panel. When you were newly pregnant, you could pretty much pull your pants up over your head. Nowadays they make maternity pants that sit under your belly, and for a lot of women, they're more comfortable. And think about pictures of your mothers and grandmothers from when they were pregnant! Ugh, maternity clothes have come a *long* way since then.

When you're pregnant, especially if you're working, you'll probably need a few items that look nice for the job. Buying maternity clothes can be pricey, so I highly recommend finding a friend from whom you can borrow things. Check out resale stores and look online at places like eBay for deals on maternity clothes as well.

I've read books and heard experts say that accessoriz-

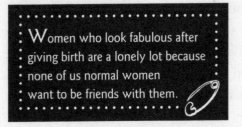

Women who look fabulous after giving birth are a lonely lot because none of us normal women want to be friends with them.

ing is the key to looking good and feeling good about yourself. Oh sure. When you're feeling like a bloated cow, a nice pair of earrings will make you feel just dandy. When you look in the mirror and see the reflection of the Stay Puft marshmallow man, a cute scarf is sure to make you feel like a million bucks. NOT! I'm sorry, but no amount of tasteful accessorizing is going to make you look or feel wonderful at this point. Women who can't fit in their clothes, are constipated, have faces that are broken out like teenagers, and whose ankles are swollen to twice their normal size don't generally perk right up with a lovely new handbag.

People will tell you that it doesn't really matter what you buy since you'll only be wearing them for a few months— and for some people this may be true. My sister was back in her regular clothes approximately seventeen minutes after giving birth. Have I mentioned how much I ~~hate~~ envy my sister? Seriously, I don't have any friends who lost all their baby weight in a matter of weeks. Women who look fabulous after giving birth are a lonely lot because none of us normal women want to be friends with them. Sounds superficial, you say? Maybe. But who would you rather be standing next to at the pool? The woman who just gave birth and is looking like a supermodel in a string bikini, or the woman who actually *looks* like she just gave birth and is wearing a huge T-shirt over her stretched-out maternity bathing suit? Just take my word on it.

For the rest of us, you might want to make sure you actually like the maternity clothes you buy, because there's a chance you'll be wearing them for a few years. But that's okay because you'll have a lot of friends. Remember, no one likes a woman who looks like she was never even pregnant a couple months after she gives birth.

Ways to Prepare for Baby

1. Get used to waking up every two hours all night long.

2. Let your dinner sit on the plate for a good half hour before sitting down to eat it.

3. Start doing eight loads of laundry every day.

4. Pretend to listen to a stranger's advice.

5. Put your name on the preschool waiting list.

6. Get used to the fact that Baby will get all the attention. Practice by telling everyone to ignore you when you walk into a crowded room.

7. Pack your bag for the hospital right away, so your husband doesn't have to pack for you should you go into labor early.

8. Consider asking a girlfriend who has already given birth to come with you to the hospital. She'll help offset the stupid things your husband will do.

9. Take all your belongings and throw them all over the family room. This is what your house will look like for the next eighteen years.

10. Go out to your car and spill juice on the seats. Scatter French fries, crayons, and toys on the floor, and put a *Veggie Tales* CD in the player.

CHAPTER 8

HALFWAY THERE!

(MONTH FIVE)

You're five months along. You're definitely pregnant. There's no denying it at this point. You look pregnant, you feel pregnant, and you should pretty well be used to the idea by now. When I was five months along with my fifth baby, Clayton, a stranger looked at me and said, "Oh, when are you due?" I told him, "Not for another four months." He did a double take and looked at me incredulously. "Seriously?" he asked. "I thought you were due this week! You're huge!" I knocked him out with a right hook to the jaw.

Besides looking obviously pregnant, you're feeling your baby move, which is a wonderful confirmation of the fact. Most of the discomforts of the first trimester are far behind you and you are most likely enjoying the energy that comes during the second trimester.

Still, there will probably be some new aches and pains that will arise around this time.

Ow, My Aching Back!

Chances are, if you haven't already, you'll start experiencing some backaches around this time. It's no wonder when you think about how your body is changing. Your growing uterus is putting strain on your lower back and can cause some big-time pain. Think about hanging a watermelon around your neck. You'd have a hard time walking around for long with that extra weight out there in front, pulling on your back.

You can help alleviate your back pain by changing position often. Don't stand or sit for too long without getting up and moving around. Wear comfortable, supportive shoes. Don't follow the whole "barefoot and pregnant" thing like I did. This can cause more back pain, not to mention foot pain and/or plantar fasciitis. Skip the flip-flops and the high heels and go for a more supportive pair of Birkenstocks, a sturdy pair of tennis shoes, or some comfy Dansko clogs. When you need to lift something heavy, make sure you do it properly. First, bend at the knees, and then call your husband or a nice strong man to lift it for you.

When sleeping, I found lying on my side with my legs curled up a bit provided the most comfort for my back. You really shouldn't sleep on your back while you're pregnant because besides being uncomfortable and causing considerable back pain, it can lower your blood pressure, causing you to get light-headed, and it can make it difficult to breathe. Of course, sleeping on your stomach while you're pregnant is out, too. Believe me, it is not comfortable to sleep on a beach ball and that's what it feels like if you try to sleep on your stomach while pregnant. The most comfortable position I found was lying on my side with about a thousand pillows surrounding me. I had a pillow beneath my head, between my knees, by my belly, and behind my back. Of course, with all those pillows, your husband may have to sleep on the floor, but that's just a sacrifice you may have to make. After you give birth, you can use the pillows to help position baby for nursing while reclining. And when your kids get a little older, they can use them to hit each other repeatedly until the stuffing comes out. Or maybe it's just my kids who do that . . .

For days when I had to spend a lot of time on my feet and my back ended up really aching in the evening, I found that relaxing in a nice warm tub helped. Well, until the kids started banging on the bathroom door anyway. You could also try placing a heating pad set on low on your aching back muscles. As always, don't take any pain relievers before consulting with your doctor.

Exercise—Just Say No

I hate to exercise when I'm not pregnant: I wasn't about to start doing it in pregnancy! As far as I'm concerned, the only reason to exercise is to lose weight and, obviously, that

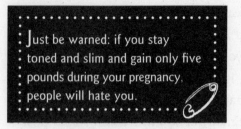

Just be warned: if you stay toned and slim and gain only five pounds during your pregnancy, people will hate you.

isn't happening when you're pregnant. I suppose there are people out there who actually like to exercise (poor misguided souls). Recently, when I was at the doctor's office being tested for bee allergies, I sat next to an older gentleman who bragged about his low blood pressure and said it was due to exercising. He said something about endorphins and feeling good and heart health and cholesterol blah blah blah. I stabbed him with my EpiPen.

Seriously, though, if you are the type of ~~weirdo~~ person who liked exercising before you became pregnant, check with your doctor about your favorite way to get your heart pumping. As long as you don't do anything too crazy or strenuous, you'll probably be given the go-ahead to continue throughout your pregnancy. Just be warned: if you stay toned and slim and gain only five pounds during your pregnancy, ~~I will~~ people will hate you. If exercise is worth that, then go ahead.

If you never really got into exercise before pregnancy, why would you want to start now? If the only time you ran prepregnancy was when someone was chasing you, why would you want to start now when you're lugging an extra ~~sixty~~ thirty-five pounds around? About the only exercise I did while pregnant was walking. Walking to the refrigerator, walking to the bathroom, walking to the couch to take a nap. Ha-ha-ha! Oh, my stomach hurts laughing at that one! Which reminds me—when you're pregnant, you can simply count laughing as your exercise for the week.

Anyway, here's the deal—your body is doing more work now than if you were lifting weights, doing aerobics, or running on a treadmill. Growing a baby is a ton of work, and you've been feeling the side effects of all this work for months. Just wait until labor and delivery. Labor and delivery will make even the hardest workouts look like a walk in the park. Besides, you'll have plenty of time to try to work off those "last ten pounds" after the baby is born. Save your strength for making your baby. And if you get the sudden urge to exercise, just lie down and take a nap until the feeling passes.

Baby's First Concert

There are some folks who believe playing music for their baby will make him or her smarter. These people will put headphones over their pregnant abdomens and play Mozart and Bach for the developing fetus. I say, why stop there? Read your baby Aristotle and Shakespeare. Do complex mathematical equations aloud, recite poetry, sing, do interpretative dance. (In case anyone's missing it, that was sarcasm.) I don't really know if there's evidence that playing music for or talking to your baby in utero will make him or her smarter, but the thought of putting a pair of headphones over my pregnant belly or reciting the collective works of Melville makes me alternate between cringing and laughing. If this is something you feel strongly about, knock yourself out, but keep it to yourself. If you share this little tidbit with your friends, they will laugh at you. And when yours is the kid in preschool who sits there eating paste, you may have to rethink the whole "playing music for my baby in utero will make him a genius" thing.

Things You Learn in Childbirth Classes

1. *How to make your pregnancy more comfortable.* They'll tell you things like "eat healthy" and "exercise." I, for one, don't equate exercising with comfort, however.

2. *How your partner can help you relax during labor.* This works only if your partner pays attention and does not lie down on the pillows and fall fast asleep.

3. *That there's always one overachiever couple in class who do everything by the book.* You can tell them apart by the fact that she glows and brags about how she's only gained five pounds thanks to her all-natural, organic diet. He'll brag that his wife is awesome and won't need any pain medication during labor. They'll smile ~~sickeningly~~ sweetly at each other. Ignore them and make friends with the ~~normal~~ other couples.

4. *Answers to your questions and concerns.* The instructor should be able to answer questions like, *Am I justified in kicking my doctor if he cuts me "down there"?*

5. *How to diaper a baby doll.* Of course, this doesn't provide experience in diapering an actual baby who kicks and squirms and occasionally pees on you.

6. *A graphic video on vaginal deliveries and C-sections.* This will almost guarantee that your husband will change his mind about wanting to be in the delivery room with you.

CHAPTER 9

FEELING FINE

(MONTH SIX)

Six months! You've made it through almost two trimesters! By the end of this month, you'll be two-thirds of the way there! You've most likely spent the last couple months feeling pretty good. You've probably enjoyed the burst of energy and the fact that you're looking pregnant, which means you're getting a lot of positive attention from friends, family, and strangers alike.

You're used to the idea that you are indeed pregnant, but as you approach your third and final trimester, the reality that you're going to have to go through labor and delivery eventually begins to sink in. You will probably spend large quantities of time fantasizing about your baby and imagining what the labor and delivery process will be like.

If you haven't yet, you'll probably want to take a childbirth class of some sort. You'll also probably want to start getting serious about picking out a name for your little one.

Hand Numbness

If you wake up one day and can't feel your hands, don't worry. This is very common in pregnancy. It's really fun when you wake up to a ringing phone and you can't make your hands work to actually grab the receiver. You just sort of swing your hands around and flop them on the phone, which knocks it off the hook and makes it crash to the floor. Or maybe you wake up to the kids asking you to pour them some milk and you quickly discover you can't actually open the milk carton.

My friend Jenny and I both experienced a lot of numbness in our hands while we were pregnant. In fact, it got so annoying and uncomfortable with my sixth pregnancy that I had to wear wrist braces to help keep my hands straight while sleeping. This numbness and tingling (and sometimes pain) is caused by carpal tunnel syndrome. Before I was pregnant, I thought the Carpal Tunnel connected midtown Manhattan to New Jersey. Little did I know that the carpal tunnel is located in your wrist, and, much like your ankles and face and pretty much everything else during pregnancy, it can swell. This puts pressure on the nerves and can make your thumb and first couple fingers numb or tingly. If you find yourself sleeping on your hands or bending them at the wrist while you sleep, discuss this with your doctor. He may recommend you wear braces to help alleviate the problem. As with most pregnancy symptoms, this usually goes away soon after giving birth.

Have a Baby, Lose a Tooth

There's a saying that goes a little something like this: Have a baby, lose a tooth. My dentist tells me I'm the poster child for this adage. I used to have nice teeth. I did, I did! And then I had kids. With each pregnancy, I developed four to six cavities. I even managed to need a root canal while I was pregnant with Clayton. I needed a crown and everything! Technically, that makes me a princess, by the way. Be prepared to have your teeth fall out of your head when you get pregnant. Some doctors will claim there's no medical proof of this, but I'm telling you that with each one of my six pregnancies, I got a whole slew of cavities. I'm not the only one, either. My sister's teeth fell apart during her pregnancy as well. In fact, I have a few friends who also had their teeth deteriorate during pregnancy, and my dentist has seen this phenomenon again and again.

Of course, if morning sickness causes you to vomit repeatedly during your pregnancy, the acids can damage the enamel on your teeth. Sometimes the nausea associated with morning sickness can keep a woman from brushing her teeth as well as she should, but even women who don't experience morning sickness can have teeth issues during or immediately after pregnancy.

By all means, keep your regular cleaning appointments, but if you encounter any dental problems while

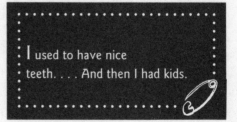

I used to have nice teeth. . . . And then I had kids.

you're pregnant, check with your obstetrician first. You'll have to weigh the pros and cons of having work done before deciding if you should go ahead now or wait until after you give birth. I think if it's at all possible, it's better to wait until after having your baby to have work done. I had an abscessed tooth when I was five or six months pregnant with my fifth baby. My gum was infected and I was in a tremendous amount of pain, so I couldn't put off my root canal until after I had my baby. My doctor gave me the green light to get the dental work done.

I lay back in the chair as my dentist shot up my gums with Novocain. He left the room and I just enjoyed the peace and quiet that comes when a mom of four young children gets out of the house by herself (even if it is a visit to the dentist). After a few seconds, I started feeling woozy. I mean, I was really feeling funky and was pretty sure I was going to pass out. There was a buzzing sound in my ears, and my vision became blurred as the room faded to black. The next thing I knew, my dentist was raising my chair to a sitting position and putting a cool, damp towel on my forehead.

I was freaked out and I think I freaked out everyone in the office as well. My dentist was thinking, *Now that's a first—a pregnant woman fainting in my office! I so did not sign up for this!*

I felt fine as long as I was sitting upright, but the minute he started to recline my chair again, the pressure of my huge uterus on my back, my intestines, and my veins made me light-headed. My dentist was nice enough to keep my chair in an upright position as he worked on my tooth while standing. I'm pretty sure he instituted a "No pregnant women allowed" rule after this incident. If you do have to get the dental work done, be prepared. If you have morning sickness, you may gag more than usual. You may not feel well after lying back for an extended period of time, either. You might want to make sure your dental insurance is up-to-date, too. That's just a heads-up from me to you. I know I'd never even considered these things when I was pregnant with my first.

Battle Scars

Ah yes, stretch marks. The good news is that there's a way to avoid them. The bad news is the way to avoid them is to avoid getting pregnant. If you're reading this book, it's probably a little too late for you. You probably already know that stretch marks come with the territory if you're pregnant. You've probably already resigned yourself to the fact that you'll have these lines crossing your abdomen. The thing about stretch marks that may surprise you, however, is that they won't only cross your belly, but they'll appear on your breasts and hips, too. They'll show up pretty much anywhere your body has expanded and stretched. And in pregnancy, your body expands and stretches everywhere but your eyeballs.

There are a hundred different lotions, potions, and creams out there that promise to prevent stretch marks. They lie. Use them if you'd like to. They won't do any harm. It's always nice to have moisturized skin, especially in the winter when your skin tends to be a bit dry, but

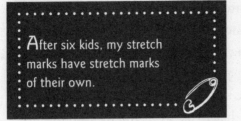

After six kids, my stretch marks have stretch marks of their own.

don't believe the lotions are any kind of magic elixir that will prevent or erase stretch marks. Even after several pregnancies, I was always amazed at how many new stretch marks I got with each subsequent pregnancy. After six kids, my stretch marks have stretch marks of their own. My advice to you is, don't worry about them. The baggy maternity clothes you'll be wearing for the ~~rest of your life~~ next few months will cover the stretch marks nicely.

Gee, Your Hair Looks Terrific!

Okay, I've written about a hundred pages of dreadful pregnancy symptoms that will probably make any sane woman decide she never wants to have children. Ever. But here's a good one! Your hair will grow like crazy! You will have beautiful hair! Oh how I miss my pregnancy hair. My hair was shiny and thick and not a single strand fell out during my entire pregnancy. Of course, after giving birth, so much hair fell out that I would think there was a small squirrel in my shower drain after washing my hair, but that's another story. If you've been wanting to grow your hair, now is your chance.

Your nails will also become longer and stronger. Even women who have always had brittle nails that easily chip will notice a difference. My nails have never looked better than when I was pregnant. I don't usually put colored polish on my nails because I hate to draw attention to them, but during my pregnancies, I sure did. That was a nice little pick-me-up, in fact. When the rest of your body feels like it's falling apart, it is nice to have pretty nails. In fact, if you can swing it, treat yourself to a professional manicure and pedicure while you're pregnant. I especially recommend the pedicure because everyone feels better with pretty toes, and trust me when I say you will not be able to reach your feet by the time you give birth. It's impossible. Don't even try. You'll look like a fool, your family will make fun of you, and you could fall over attempting to reach them. I know this from experience. That's me—doing stupid things so you don't have to.

Boobs, hair, and nails—these are the perks of pregnancy. Enjoy them while they last.

Bleeding Noses and Gums

You finally get over the nausea that has hit every time you brushed your teeth for the past several months, and now when you brush your teeth, your gums start bleeding. This is just another way your body is trying to make you stop brushing so you'll need a root canal by the time you give birth.

Actually, this is another common pregnancy symptom. Your

Boobs, hair, and nails—these are the perks of pregnancy. Enjoy them while they last.

gums, like every other part of your body, swell and can bleed during brushing. It's okay. Just try to brush a little more gently through the duration of your pregnancy. Make sure you have a nice, soft-bristled toothbrush, and make sure to brush and floss regularly. If your gums bleed while brushing, try rinsing your mouth with cold water when you've finished to help stop any bleeding.

I also got nosebleeds now and then when I was pregnant. These were more frequent during the winter months when the heat was on and the house was really dry. If you find that your nose is really dry, you can use some plain saline drops to help moisten your nasal passages. If you get a nosebleed, try leaning forward a bit and simply pinch your nose for a couple minutes so the blood doesn't drip down your throat. Or you could stick a couple tampons up your nose since you're not using them for anything else these days.

Besides the occasional nosebleed, my friends and I all experienced a huge amount of stuffiness. We felt like we had head colds for the last few months of pregnancy. The bad news is that it will likely continue to get worse throughout your pregnancy. The good news is that it will magically disappear very soon after giving birth. You can try using a humidifier or neti pot to ease the congestion. Sometimes taking a warm shower can help break up some nasal congestion, but don't go taking any decongestants or other medications without your doctor's okay. This is just one of those things you'll have to deal with until you give birth.

You Mean, All I Have to Do Is Breathe???

At some point in your pregnancy, you'll probably at least consider taking a childbirth class. I'm here to tell you all about what you'll learn in this kind of class and to explain why these classes can sometimes lead to divorce.

My husband and I took a Lamaze class when I was pregnant with Austin, my first baby. We wanted to be prepared and were eager to learn whatever we could to make labor, delivery, and caring for our newborn go as smoothly as possible. Actually, it turned out that I was the only one who wanted to learn as much as I could to make labor and delivery and caring for my newborn go as smoothly as possible. My husband wanted to goof off and act like an idiot there.

In this class, I learned about the different stages of labor and what the typical woman experiences during each stage. I learned about vaginal deliveries and C-sections. I learned about pain-relief options and what most women experience postpartum. I also learned how to bathe, diaper, and feed a baby. My husband learned that lying back on the pillows and dozing off during a film about childbirth can make a pregnant woman angry. He learned that goofing off and playing with the baby doll when he's supposed to be diapering it can make a pregnant woman angry. He also learned that an angry pregnant woman can hit really hard.

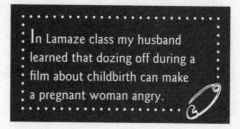

In Lamaze class my husband learned that dozing off during a film about childbirth can make a pregnant woman angry.

Honestly, I think the class was useful because I believe in being prepared. I liked hearing about different childbirth scenarios, and I found the information about pain relief useful. I listened intently to the part about C-sections, because you just never know. C-sections are always a possibility even if you aren't planning on having one, so I think you should be prepared just in case. It'll make it less frightening if you do end up needing one in the end.

However, the part about breathing? Well, that was just ridiculous.

"Breathe like this," the instructor said as she demonstrated, Bill Cosby–style, how to breathe through labor pain.

At the time, I took notes. I believed everything she said. If the instructor says all I have to do is breathe and I won't need any pain medication, then all I have to do is breathe. How wonderful! I'm so glad I'm taking this class. Of course, after I was in labor for ten minutes with my first baby, I realized she was lying! It doesn't matter how you breathe, labor hurts. The only way breathing exercises will do away with labor pain is if you hyperventilate and pass out. And even then, I'm guessing you'll probably still feel pain, despite the fact that you're passed out cold.

So, in the end, take the class. Listen to the instructor. Soak up as much information as you can. And try to choke back your laughter when she tells you that labor won't hurt if you just breathe. Oh yeah, and have a talk with your husband before you leave the house. Tell him that the pillows are for *you*! And that he should not, under any circumstances, fall asleep during any part of the class. Oh yeah, and the baby doll is *not* a toy!

Baby Items You Must Have

1. *A swing.* Five of my six babies spent a good deal of time in their swings.

2. *Car seat cover.* This is a definite must for those living in climates with cold winters.

3. *Cloth diapers.* These not only cover Baby's butt, they're great burp rags, and when Baby's older, they can be turned into dusting cloths or cleaning rags.

4. *Onesies.* These are the uniform of babies everywhere.

5. *Diaper cream.* At some point your baby is bound to get diaper rash, and this is a lifesaver. Plus, your toddler can smear it into the carpet to ensure you have lasting memories of his babyhood.

6. *A good, sturdy, roomy diaper bag.* Even when Baby outgrows the need for a diaper bag, you can use it to pack stuff for jaunts to the park or beach or Grandma's house.

7. *Diapers.* This one's kinda obvious.

8. *A bouncy seat.* These can soothe even the fussiest of babies.

9. *Baby album.* This usually applies only to your first child, possibly your second.

10. *Stroller.* I not only used mine taking my babies for walks, but after my babies were grown, I used it when shopping at the mall. It's a great place to pile up your packages so you can shop hands-free.

CHAPTER 10

IN THE HOME STRETCH

(MONTH SEVEN)

Y ou're seven months now! Hooray. You'll probably start counting down days at this point (if you
haven't already). When people you haven't seen for a while
ask you, "Wow! You *still* haven't had that baby yet?" you
will feel that kicking them is a perfectly reasonable reaction.
You're getting a little tired of this whole pregnancy yourself, and you don't need to be reminded about how you're
still pregnant. Some days you'll probably wonder if you'll be
pregnant for the rest of your life.

At this point, besides getting tired of being pregnant,
most women start to feel tired and uncomfortable. Unless,
of course, you're my sister or sister-in-law, in which case,
you're just glowing and have never felt better in your life. I
~~hate~~ am so happy for my sister and sister-in-law.

You've taken a class on childbirth so you technically
know what's going to happen, but you'll still probably do

a lot of dreaming and fantasizing about labor and delivery. You've probably read *What to Expect When You're Expecting* from cover to cover at least eighteen times by now. Here's what I have to say about this month.

My Feet Are the Size of the Grand Canyon (and could hold as much water, too!)

Ah, yes, the swollen feet. I remember this well. Pretty much every body part you have will swell during pregnancy. Your feet oftentimes suffer the worst. With my fifth and sixth pregnancies, because I had such awful varicose veins in my left leg, my left foot swelled a lot. My veins didn't work as well as they should to pump fluid back up and it accumulated in my ankle. I had to loosen the straps on my left sandal two notches more than the right one in order to fit my swollen foot. I probably looked like Frankenstein's monster lurching around with my different-sized shoes. Most mornings, when I first woke up, the swelling had subsided, but by the afternoon, my foot was puffed up again. I have friends who could wear only sandals even in the dead of winter because they just couldn't cram their feet into their regular shoes.

And it's not just your ankles that swell. Sometimes your hands do, too. My friends Amy and Jenny even had to have their wedding rings cut off. If you find your wedding band getting tight, please take it off and put it away until after delivery. As much as you hate to take it off, believe me, it'll make you even more sad to have it cut off because you no longer have any circulation in your finger.

It's normal to ex-
perience some swell-
ing in your ankles. If
the swelling is severe,
if it doesn't go down
at night when you're

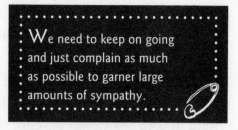

We need to keep on going
and just complain as much
as possible to garner large
amounts of sympathy.

resting, or if it's accompanied by swelling in your hands or
face, high blood pressure, or protein in the urine (signs the
doctor will look for at your appointments), it could indicate
the beginning of preeclampsia. Call your doctor right away if
your swelling persists or if you notice swelling in your hands
and/or face.

For most of us, swollen ankles are just a nuisance. Try,
if at all possible, to prop up your feet at work if you can.
If you're home with small children, pop in a movie for the
little ones and elevate your feet by stretching out on the
couch. I just crack myself up every time I give the advice
of lying down or taking it easy or propping up your feet. I
don't know why I keep writing this when I know very well
that it's not a possibility for moms who already have small
children. I guess I keep writing it because it sounds good. In
an ideal world, it would be nice to take it easy, but we moms
know that just isn't practical. If we lie down to rest, we take
a chance that our other children will burn down the house.
Realistically, we need to keep on going and just complain as
much as possible to garner large amounts of sympathy.

Also, make sure you drink enough water. I know, I
know, it seems like drinking water would be the last thing
you'd want to do, right? I mean, do you really want to
add *more* fluids to your body? But drinking plenty of water

(eight to ten glasses each day, just like when you're dieting) will help flush out excess fluids. I don't know how it works, but it does.

If you push on your ankle and it leaves an indentation, that's not a good sign. I mean, it's kinda fun to make designs in your ankles and calves by pushing your thumb into your skin, but swelling that severe can be a sign of serious problems, so you should probably stop trying to "write" your name on your leg and call your doctor right away.

Can Someone Turn on the Air-Conditioning Already?!

While you're pregnant, your internal thermostat will be in overdrive. If you're pregnant in the summer, be prepared to melt. If you're pregnant in the spring, be prepared to melt. If you're pregnant in the fall, be prepared to melt. If you're pregnant in the winter, well, be prepared to melt then, too. I remember walking to pick up my kids from school in the dead of winter wearing only a sweatshirt. (We live in Chicago, where it drops to ninety below in the winter.) My friend Ginny, who would be bundled up like an Eskimo, would look at me like I was crazy. I was always warm. When I was pregnant during the summer with my first baby, we didn't have air-conditioning in our house. I frequently called my parents in the evening, "So whatcha doing? Wouldn't you like some company tonight? I bet you really miss me, huh? I could come over and hang out with you guys. Really, I don't mind at all." The fact that I felt the need to visit my parents so much had nothing to do with the fact that they had central air. Honest.

The key to surviving is to take fourteen showers a day. Use several layers of deodorant and sprinkle generously with powder. You also want to make sure you dress in layers in the winter so you can discard everything but your underwear when you heat up. In the summer, just run around naked. Okay, that might not be the best suggestion. A bikini should do the trick. Just don't leave the house.

My husband got fed up with me by the end of each of my pregnancies because I insisted on sleeping with the windows open and/or the air-conditioning blasting and the fan on full speed over the bed. The poor guy lay there shivering under a huge pile of blankets while I lay uncovered and sweating. But a girl's gotta do what a girl's gotta do.

Such a Pain in My Butt

If you experience pain that starts in your lower back and radiates down through your butt and into your leg, it very well may be sciatica. Sciatica is just a fancy word for "UNBELIEVABLY HORRENDOUS PAIN IN YOUR BUTT, BACK, AND LEG!" It happens when the growing uterus puts pressure on the sciatic nerve. This causes pain and sometimes numbness and/or tingling, too. There are varying degrees to which this can affect you. I think I experienced some amount of sciatica with each of my six pregnancies. (Then again, thanks to that blissful pregnancy amnesia, I'm not positive about this.)

Usually, if I treated the pain with a heating pad or a warm bath, it would go away after a couple days.

When I was pregnant with Lexi, my fourth baby, however, the sciatica I had was awful. It was debilitating. I couldn't move off the couch for several days. I literally cried every time I had to get up to go to the bathroom, and being pregnant with a bladder the size of a pistachio meant I had to go often. My doctor finally had to prescribe me pain medication so I could move at all. The pain medicine helped, but I still couldn't get up and walk for several days. Finally after a week, my baby shifted and the pressure on my sciatic nerve eased up, and I was once again able to move.

The more I write about the discomforts of pregnancy, the more I wonder why I purposely went through this *six* times! What person in her right mind would do this? You wouldn't hit your thumb with a hammer and say, *Hmm, I think I'll do that again. And again. And again. And again. And again.* That's just crazy! Then again, you don't get a beautiful little baby to love when you hit yourself with a hammer. I guess that's why I, and countless others, go on to have more than one child. Well, that and the blessed pregnancy amnesia.

Anyway, if you experience sciatic pain, try applying a heating pad set on low or medium to your lower back. You can also try changing positions. Sometimes just moving around or lying on your side or standing on your head with one arm pointing west and one leg bent at a forty-five-degree angle does the trick. If the pain becomes unbearable or incapacitates you, give your doctor a call. And, as always, use this as an excuse to get out of cooking, cleaning, and doing anything more strenuous than lying around watching the Food Network for hours on end.

Kickboxing 101

Somewhere along this time, your baby's legs become as powerful as a kangaroo's. Those sweet little flutters you first felt several months ago will be replaced by karate kicks that would leave Mr. Miyagi impressed. You, on the other hand, will be in too much pain to be impressed. When your sweet little baby jams his foot up in your rib cage, you'll wish for those feathery light movements of months past.

Sometimes your baby will move and hit you right in the cervix. This is painful. This is very painful. On more than one occasion, I was just walking along, minding my own business only to get kicked down low in my uterus. I remember looking down, fully expecting to see a foot hanging out. You'll be surprised at how much kicking one tiny little baby can do.

They have to kick like this in utero. It's practice for after they're born and it's time to change their diapers. It's Baby's job to make diaper changing a physical challenge for you. The more they kick and squirm, the harder it is to hold on to their tiny ankles and the more likely you are to smear the diaper's contents all over the

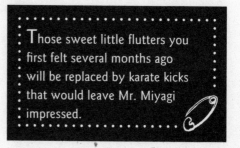

Those sweet little flutters you first felt several months ago will be replaced by karate kicks that would leave Mr. Miyagi impressed.

changing table, Baby's legs, two or three of Baby's outfits, your hands, your arms, your shirt, the wall . . .

Sometimes changing your position can stop your little one from kickboxing for a while. Getting up and walking around or lying down might help. If switching positions doesn't do the trick and Junior insists on trying to kick his way out, just remember this, it's worse when Junior is five years old, wakes up because there's a thunderstorm, crawls into bed with you, and kicks you in the back all night. Five-year-old legs are generally stronger than a four-pound fetus's legs. So, look on the bright side!

One day you'll miss the in-utero squirming and kicking. I know, I know, it's hard to believe. I wouldn't have believed it either back when I was pregnant with my first, but after I gave birth, that is the one thing I missed about pregnancy. It was just strange not to feel anyone moving around inside me.

Baby Items You'll Never Need

1. *A wipe warmer.* Really, how cold do wipes get sitting in your room-temperature house?

2. *The 50,000 receiving blankets you'll get as gifts.* More than one or two hundred is really not necessary.

3. *Fancy-schmancy diaper pails.* There are a hundred and one diaper pails out there designed to keep diaper stink in. Over time, no matter how wonderful the pails are, the stink will escape and permeate everything in your house. It's best to promptly throw diapers out the door and into your neighbor's yard.

4. *A bottle sterilizer.* You already have one of these. It's called a dishwasher.

5. *A dozen pacifiers.* With my first couple babies, I had dozens of pacifiers to offer them. You really don't need a ton until you know if your baby will use one. And then you'll need at least four hundred because they will get lost daily.

6. *Knee pads to protect Baby's widdle knees when they're learning to crawl.* Completely ridiculous.

7. *A thermometer for Baby's bath.* You don't really need this as long as you have the ability to *feel the water with your hand and see if it's too hot!*

8. *A bassinet.* Sure it's cute, but Baby will outgrow it in approximately two and a half hours.

CHAPTER 11

ALMOST THERE

(MONTH EIGHT)

Y ou're in the home stretch! Eight months. The countdown begins in earnest now. Basically, by the time you get to this point, you will feel like you have been pregnant for twenty years. You will want the baby out. NOW! As you're nearing the end of your pregnancy, you'll probably find yourself daydreaming about your baby more and more. You'll lie awake at night playing out labor-and-delivery scenes in your mind. You'll imagine what your baby will look like. You'll worry about taking him home and not knowing how to care for him.

Adding to the growing impatience for the pregnancy to be over are the aches and pains you'll surely experience. As your belly expands, it puts more and more pressure on, well, pretty much every part of your body. Have you ever seen a diagram of a pregnant woman's torso? As Baby gets bigger, all your other organs get squished out of place. It really is a wonder that women can carry a baby; provide a safe home in which it can grow and develop; and when it's time, give birth to it. It is truly a miracle and a wonderful gift from God. Now, keep this in mind when you run out of breath while walking out to your car, you develop hemorrhoids, your ankles swell, and your back aches. Seriously, keep the wonder of it all in mind and remember it—or you'll end your day in tears. That's pretty much how the eighth month goes.

I Can't Breathe

By the time I was this far along, I'd have to stop to catch my breath whenever I'd leave the mall or work and walk through the parking lot to my car. If this happens to you, it doesn't necessarily mean you're out of shape. I mean, you might be. I certainly was by the time I got to my fifth and sixth pregnancies. Oh, who am I kidding? I was out of shape going into my first pregnancy! But the shortness of breath that pregnant women often experience doesn't mean you aren't physically fit. As Baby grows bigger, your uterus expands and pushes up against your diaphragm. Your lungs end up ~~the size of grape tomatoes~~ getting a bit squished in the process. Because your lung capacity is ~~gone~~ a little diminished, you can find it hard to get a full breath.

Of course, lugging around an extra twenty pounds or so (or an extra fifty pounds, if you're like me and gained enough weight to support eight babies) can leave you a bit winded as well.

I didn't even have to do anything physical to get winded. Late in pregnancy, simply talking left me breathless. I'd have to catch my breath while just sitting on the couch and chatting with a friend on the phone. My friends on the other end of the line would ask me, "Are you okay? What are you doing? You sound so out of breath!" I couldn't very well tell them that I was just sitting on the couch eating chocolate chip cookies, now, could I? "Oh, I was exercising. Just got finished jogging five miles, in fact."

I could just see my friends rolling their eyes and thinking, *Yeah right! Dawn jogging five miles! Good one! Maybe if you didn't talk so much, making up your stories, Dawn, you wouldn't have such a hard time breathing.*

I didn't notice the shortness of breath too much with my first two pregnancies, but by the time I was about six months pregnant with Jackson, my third baby, I was having a really hard time breathing. In fact, my doctor even prescribed an inhaler for me. I never actually had to use it, but I had a tough time getting a good full breath throughout the last trimester. (Same thing happened in my subsequent pregnancies, too.)

So, if you find yourself a bit more winded these days, mention it to your doctor but don't worry about it. If you're having a very difficult time breathing, you don't feel well, and/or your lips and fingers are turning blue, ~~use it as an excuse to get out of as much work as possible~~ call your doctor immediately.

Is That a Contraction or Are You Just Happy to Tease Me?

Braxton Hicks contractions are just your body's way of sticking out its tongue at you and saying neener neener neener! Just when you think you're having contractions and labor must be starting, that's when these Braxton Hicks contractions say, "Ha-ha! Fooled ya! You're not in labor! Ha!"

I remember feeling these practice contractions during my first pregnancy and thinking, *Okay, these aren't too painful. Why do women complain about labor so much? I can handle this!* In other words, I was a total fool. Braxton Hicks contractions are like real contractions in the way that your kitchen faucet is like Niagara Falls. You'll feel your uterus tighten, but Braxton Hicks contractions aren't painful like real ones. These are just nature's way of getting your uterus ready for the real contractions that will follow in a couple months.

As you near your ninth month, the Braxton Hicks contractions come more frequently and are more intense. This can make first-time moms (and even seasoned veterans) wonder if they're in real labor or not. It can be difficult to distinguish. If you aren't due yet and you're experiencing contractions that happen more than four times an hour, contractions that are painful, or contractions along with a bloody discharge, call your doctor. It may just be Braxton Hicks contractions, but you'll probably need to go to the hospital so the entire nursing staff can laugh at you and point out the fact that you can't distinguish real labor from Braxton Hicks contractions.

When I was pregnant with Jackson, I went to the hospital not once, but *twice* in false labor. It was my *third* baby! How could a woman who has gone through labor and delivery twice already not know if she's actually in labor, right? On my first false-labor visit, I was monitored for a

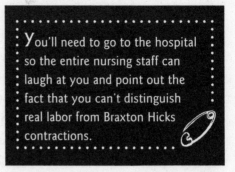

You'll need to go to the hospital so the entire nursing staff can laugh at you and point out the fact that you can't distinguish real labor from Braxton Hicks contractions.

while, then sent home from the hospital and told to come back when I was really in labor. As I recall, the nurses were nice and reassuring and told me stuff like, "This happens all the time. Don't worry about it. You're certainly not the first woman, nor will you be the last, to mistake Braxton Hicks contractions for real labor. Now go home and don't come back and bug us until you're actually in labor, you crazy woman who cried ~~wolf~~ labor."

I went home, sad, depressed, overdue with my baby, still pregnant, and feeling like an idiot for thinking I was in labor when I wasn't. After several hours at home, I was certain that my contractions had gotten more intense and I was without a doubt, definitely in labor this time, so I headed back to the hospital again. And once again, I was told ~~I was an idiot~~ I wasn't in labor and sent home. I'm telling you this because apparently I have no shame. I could've kept this little tidbit to myself and the world would never have known that I'd mistaken false labor for real labor twice. But I want you to know that you're not an idiot if you mistake false labor for the real thing. And even though you probably feel like an idiot, you're in good company because there are many of us who have done the same thing. It can be our little secret.

I always liked feeling those Braxton Hicks contractions because, in my mind, they were helping to dilate my cervix. It didn't matter that week after week, I'd go to my doctor and she would say, "Nope, you ~~still~~ aren't dilated at all." I still believed that somehow these contractions were really working to get labor started. Have I mentioned that pregnant women sometimes fantasize? But speaking of dilating—don't let your early dilatation (or lack thereof) concern you. In my experience, it doesn't really matter if you start to dilate before you go into labor or not. I hadn't dilated even one centimeter when I went into labor with Lexi, for example, yet my labor with her was very fast. You might think that if you're already dilated two or three centimeters when you go into labor, it might be faster and easier. This isn't always the case. Conversely, if you aren't dilated at all when you go into labor, it doesn't necessarily mean that you'll have a long, drawn-out labor. You just never know. And when that stranger on the subway, after asking how much you're dilated, tells you that you'll have a fast (or slow) labor, just say that you've already scheduled your labor to last precisely four hours. No, of course, you can't schedule your labor to last for a certain amount of time, but it's fun to watch the all-knowing stranger's puzzled expression.

Presentation

I'm not talking about a big demonstration you put together for work here. *Presentation* refers to the position your baby is in. At your regular doctor's appointments, your physi-

cian will feel your abdomen to see if Baby's head is pointing down yet. I always thought it was kind of fun trying to
figure out which way my baby was lying. Usually I could
tell when my baby had turned upside down because I'd feel
more kicking up in my ribs. By squishing your tummy, your
doctor should be able to tell which direction your baby is
pointing. If your baby hasn't flipped down in the eighth
month, don't worry about it. Sometimes babies like to take
their own sweet time turning around. And some babies are
especially difficult and don't like to flip over at all. Sometimes those same babies turn into stubborn toddlers who
like to do things their own way, in their own sweet time.
Not that I ever had one of *those* babies—*cough cough Brooklyn!* If this happens to you, your physician may be able to
turn your baby manually by pressing on your abdomen. Or
you could try standing on your head or telling your baby to
"head toward the light" or drinking a whole glass of water
and holding your breath for thirty seconds. Oh wait, that
last one was for getting rid of the hiccups. Well, you could
give it a try anyway. It might work. Hey, I never claimed to
be a doctor.

Peeing Your Pants

Your baby has officially taken over your body. All your internal organs are completely squished out of place. Your lungs
are now the size of walnuts and they're up by your throat.
Your bladder is now your baby's ottoman. Or, if your baby
has turned and is pointing down, your bladder is Junior's

pillow. In either case, your bladder is a nice soft squishy thing that your baby will like to lie on. Much like in the first trimester, you'll probably find yourself running to the bathroom four thousand times a day.

Occasionally, you might possibly, perhaps, find yourself leaking urine. The more babies you've had, the more likely this is. Pregnancy does something to your bladder control, in that you no longer have any. If you don't want to carry around a change of underwear, all you have to do is avoid laughing. And coughing. And drinking more than one half ounce at a time. And uncrossing your legs. Yep, that should do it. You'll be just fine if you follow my advice. Oh, and be prepared to get up at least fifteen times a night to pee. It just happens. If you're out in public and something unexpected happens to make you laugh and you pee in your pants, just tell everyone your water broke. They'll have no idea. Then quickly leave the store and run home.

Must. Clean. Now!

Nesting is a strange phenomenon that happens to many pregnant women toward the end of their pregnancy. You know how birds gather feathers and straw and fluff and stuff

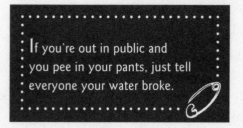
If you're out in public and you pee in your pants, just tell everyone your water broke.

to prepare their nests for their baby birds? Human moms-to-be do the same thing. Well, actually it's not quite the same thing. I mean, it would be pretty weird if we dragged a bunch of feathers, straw, and scraps of yarn into our houses and lined our baby's crib with it. But pregnant humans do often go through a spurt of energy where they have an uncontrollable urge to clean the house.

This happened to me with each and every pregnancy. I just couldn't help myself. I felt like I just *had* to organize my pantry and alphabetize my cans of soup. I had an absolute *need* to wash the walls and refold all the towels in my linen closet. My socks *had* to be lined up by color, my closets cleaned out, and my DVDS alphabetized. And let's not forget about the nursery! The diapers had to be stacked, all the clothes had to be washed in baby detergent and hung according to size, the pacifiers had to be sterilized, and the crib had to be made up just so.

Not only did I obsessively clean and organize toward the end of each of my pregnancies, but I would sit in the middle of the nursery and simply admire how everything was so neat and tidy and ready for Baby. I'd touch the tiny diapers, which were stacked in neat rows. I'd rearrange the stuffed animals propped up on the toy box. I'd look at the baskets of toiletries on the changing table and imagine the baby who would soon be sleeping in the perfectly made crib.

Well, actually I did that for only the first couple babies because after I had a couple toddlers in the house, I couldn't manage to keep anything neat and tidy to save my life. Nowadays, I rarely have the urge to do any deep cleaning because I know the kids are going to trash it in a matter of minutes. My house is only clean from about midnight until seven in the morning, when the kids wake up and start dragging out every toy they own. Truly, it's amazing how quickly a couple kids can destroy everything you've cleaned. My sons' room can be spotless when they go to bed, and by the time they wake up, the floor is buried knee-deep in *stuff*. How does it happen? HOW? This, along with where all the single socks go, is one of life's great mysteries. Enjoy your pregnancy nesting urge. Enjoy how clean and organized your home is. Take pictures, in fact, because it'll never look like this again.

Shower Me

At some point during your pregnancy, someone will most likely throw a baby shower for you. A baby shower is an event where women gather and eat little food and ooooh and ahhhh over little clothes and little diapers and little toys and little pink and blue decorations. The point of this gathering is to shower the mother-to-be with essential items she will need to care for her baby.

This is how it works. Before the actual shower, the pregnant woman drags her husband out to the baby store, where she spends eight and a half hours looking at assorted baby paraphernalia. She makes a list of everything she wants, everything her friends tell her she needs, and, what the heck, two of everything else in the store just for good measure. The father-to-be trudges behind, becoming increasingly overwhelmed by all the baby stuff he never knew he'd need. By the end of the trip, the father comes to the realization that he is no longer king of his castle. There's a new ruler in town, one who hasn't even been born yet! And his castle will not be his peaceful abode for much longer; it will slowly turn into a giant Toys "R" Us.

On the day of the actual shower, you may be tempted to bring the father-to-be along with you. Resist the urge and don't do it. Leave him at home. Trust me on this. He doesn't care about tiny baby booties. He doesn't need to see every tiny outfit you unwrap. He doesn't care what the baby lotion smells like, what a bumper pad is used for, or why you need a rectal thermometer to take Baby's temperature. He will look at the breast pump, wonder how it works, maybe play with it for a minute, and undoubtedly embarrass you. With your pregnancy hormones running rampant, you'll end the day in tears when he doesn't get as excited as you are over the cute little hooded towel with the ducks embroidered on it. Instead, leave him at home during the shower, and when he comes to pick you up, make him feel strong and virile for filling the car with your haul. Then praise his manly ability to put together a crib with his bare hands, a dozen tools, two hundred pages of instructions, three Band-Aids, and a string of choice words, muttered under his breath when "tab A" doesn't fit into "slot B."

Instead of ~~torturing your husband~~ sharing the day with your husband, enjoy the time with your female friends and relatives. They'll nibble the tiny sandwiches with the crusts cut off and drink the pink lemonade, and won't even *think* of asking for a plate of roast beef and potatoes. They'll ooooh and

> On the day of the shower, you may be tempted to bring the father-to-be along with you. Resist the urge and don't do it

aaaah at the right moments, and their conversations will be generously peppered with the phrases, "Isn't that just darling?" and "How precious!" as the expecting mother opens the gifts.

Actually, *most* of the guests will ooooh and ahhhh over the gifts; however, there will always be a couple older guests who will marvel at "the things *they've* come up with." I'm not sure who *they* are, but clearly they've come up with some ridiculous stuff according to these older shower guests. "Back in my day, we didn't have any of this fancy stuff. We had a blanket. That's it. That's all we needed for our babies. We could fold the blanket into a hooded towel, a play yard, or a diaper. We didn't have toys back then. We didn't need them. We entertained our babies with pots and pans until they were old enough to put to work. We didn't have any of these fancy car seats and disposable diapers and bottle warmers and Diaper Genies. You moms have it so easy today."

I guess you can't really blame them. I mean, the changes in baby equipment just between my first and sixth babies is incredible. My friends and I were recently talking about baby swings. My friend Denise was talking about how frequently you need to replace the batteries in baby swings. Another friend, Nancy, commented on the fact that baby swings are now made to plug into a wall outlet and you don't even need batteries. A third friend, Jane, recalled how her first swing had a crank that had to be wound by hand. I think if my grandmother had gotten into the conversation, she would have said, "Swings! Humph! Back in my day, we had to hold our babies in our arms and rock them back and forth. There was no putting them in a swing so we could cook dinner, oh no. We had to cook with our feet as we held our babies."

Oftentimes, the hostess of the shower will plan games to play. The games are always silly, embarrassing, or just plain ridiculous. Some of the more popular shower games I've played over the years have been the game where everyone is given a paper with lines of seemingly random letters on it. You have to unscramble the letters to spell out baby-related words. Unless you're less than five years old, this game is ridiculously easy. O T L T B E

Another game I've played at showers, which really has nothing to do with babies, is one where everyone takes out her purse. The hostess then calls out an item and everyone rushes to see if they can find said item in her purse. Driver's license, pen, dime, lipstick. No problem. Pretty much everyone has those items. Then the hostess will continue calling out items. This game really separates the moms of little kids from all the other women there. It's the moms of little kids who always win this game as the hostess continues. Band-Aid, aspirin, paper clip, coupon, hand sanitizer, diaper, Matchbox car, Barbie shoe, the cap from a water bottle, a used tissue with a wad of gum spit into the corner, a plastic toy hippo, a baseball card that went through the wash, some dried dandelions the kids picked and handed to the mom while she was talking to another mom, so she shoved them in her purse, and a fruit snack that's covered in lint and stuck to a quarter. . . .

An especially embarrassing game that my own mother made me play at my baby shower doesn't have a name. I think she just made it up to make me look like a fool.

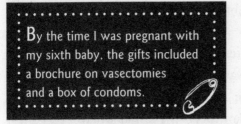

By the time I was pregnant with my sixth baby, the gifts included a brochure on vasectomies and a box of condoms.

She put an orange in the leg of a pair of pantyhose. She tied the other leg around my big ole belly. The leg with the orange dangled just above the floor. The object of this game was for me to ~~entertain everyone at the party by looking like an idiot~~ hit a golf ball with the orange in the leg of the pantyhose by swinging my hips around.

I planned a game for my sister's shower a few years ago that I thought at the time would be fun. In retrospect, I realize it was ~~really~~ just a little gross. I melted several different candy bars into diapers. I labeled each diaper and had everyone guess what kind of candy bar was in each diaper. It got a little disgusting when one guest stuck her finger in the chocolate "poo" to taste it before making her guess.

A big mistake women make is assuming that they'll have a baby shower with each pregnancy. Generally, showers are only given for first pregnancies. So, when you decide you're done having babies after your fourth one and you give away all your baby paraphernalia, you'll be out of luck when you suddenly find yourself pregnant with (surprise!) number five. And the best way to ensure you'll get pregnant is to give away all your baby stuff and maternity clothes. It works like a charm every time.

Although I didn't have a shower with my subsequent babies, my friends and family usually surprised me with gifts for them. Of course, by the time I was pregnant with my sixth baby, the gifts included a brochure on vasectomies and a box of condoms, but still, it's the thought that counts, right?

So, if you're throwing a shower for someone, don't make the mom-to-be wear a pair of pantyhose stuffed with citrus fruit around her waist. If you're attending a shower, make sure you bring your big "mom purse" so you can win that party game. And if you're the guest of honor at a shower, thank everyone profusely for arranging the party and showering you with gifts, because if you had to go out and buy all that stuff, you would need to take out a second mortgage!

Best ~~Lies~~ Ways to Get Labor Started

1. Walk
2. Eat Chinese food
3. Take castor oil
4. Sex
5. Nipple stimulation
6. Going for a bumpy car ride
7. Eating spicy food
8. Drinking raspberry leaf tea
9. Eating pineapple
10. Acupressure

CHAPTER 12

THE END IS IN SIGHT!

(MONTH NINE)

N ine months! You did it! In a couple weeks, you'll have survived nine whole months of pregnancy! This is it. Your baby could come any day now. When I got to this point with my first baby, I stopped feeling eager and started feeling scared. There's no turning back now. I'm really going to have a baby! My life is never going to be the same again! I spent a lot of time worrying about childbirth. What if my water breaks while I'm at the grocery store? What if I poop on the table while I'm pushing my baby out? (That was a huge worry of mine with my first pregnancy. I was seriously scared to death that I was going to poop while delivering my baby and my doctor would be so grossed out, he would announce to everyone in the entire maternity ward how disgusting I was.) I worried about not being able to breastfeed and not knowing how to take care of my baby once I had him. I worried that I wouldn't be able to handle the pain of childbirth, and I worried about the health and well-being of my new baby.

These are all perfectly normal feelings. They have to be; otherwise it would make me weird. And I'm not. Weird. You may experience these or other feelings similar to these. But never fear, you won't spend too much more time worrying because D-Day is almost here! Hooray!

What to Take to the Hospital

At some point, you'll need to pack a bag to take to the hospital. I always packed when I was about five months along in the hope that the simple act of packing would help speed along the last four months. It never worked.

Here's my handy list of must-haves for the hospital.

SOMETHING TO OCCUPY YOU DURING THE EARLY STAGES OF LABOR. Labor, especially for first-time moms, lasts two and a half weeks. Or so it feels. You might bring a book to read. I brought a deck of cards when I was in labor with a few of my kiddos. I found playing solitaire to be relaxing. Bring books of crossword or Sudoku puzzles if you like them, but that's like doing homework, in my opinion. I didn't like doing homework when I was in school. There was no way I was going to do math problems while in labor. I personally didn't want to use my brain any more than necessary when I was in labor, so I stuck to watching TV and reading light novels. Still, in case there's nothing on TV, or in case your husband takes over the remote and insists on watching the Bulls play-offs—despite the fact that you're in labor with *his* baby and you hate basketball (I'm still cursing Joe *and* Michael Jordan for this)—it would be a good idea to have a backup.

> Labor, especially for first-time moms, lasts like two and a half weeks.

AN MP3 PLAYER IS ANOTHER GOOD ITEM TO BRING. Listening to music can be really soothing when the contractions get painful. It can also be wonderful for tuning out your husband when he says stupid stuff like, "Does that hurt?"

I personally found no use for pen and paper. I didn't bring thank-you notes or birth announcements to address. I didn't bring a journal to record my every feeling (although, I must admit that I kind of wish I had). I didn't bring any books on caring for Baby or breastfeeding. When I was in the hospital, I didn't want to do anything akin to work, and addressing announcements or reading up on breastfeeding is like work, in my book. Some people may disagree with me (it's happened a time or two), but my friends and I were too busy concentrating on having a baby while we were in labor and then we were too wrapped up in our new little bundles afterward to want to read or write.

A CAMERA! You must, must, must bring a camera or video camera. Because of malpractice suits, most hospitals and doctors no longer let you film the birth. A lot of them don't even let you take pictures of the birth, in fact. This has changed a lot over the years. When I had my first three babies, we filmed the births (from the waist up, of course!). We snapped pictures throughout labor and delivery. When I had my fourth baby, we were instructed that we couldn't film anything until after the baby was born and we were given the okay. We were allowed to take pictures (from the waist up) during the birth. With my last two babies, we weren't allowed to film anything or take any pictures until the babies were five years old (which would explain why their baby books are so empty compared to the other kids').

Different hospitals and doctors have different rules. Check them out ahead of time so you won't be surprised or disappointed when it comes time for delivery. Still, even if your hospital doesn't allow videotaping the birth, you'll want a camera to take pictures throughout your stay at the hospital. This may seem obvious, but I'm writing this for pregnant women with "baby brain," so I need to mention simple things like batteries. Charge up your batteries and/ or bring extras. Make sure you've cleared the memory card and have plenty of space on it or bring a spare. If you're using a film camera, make sure you have several rolls. You'll be amazed at how many pictures you take from now on. By the time you leave the hospital, you'll have pictures of Junior sleeping, sort of asleep, mostly asleep, beginning to wake up, awake, starting to doze off, eyes open, eyes closed, eyes half open, mouth open, yawning, moving his little hands, suck-ing his thumb, sucking his finger, with a hat on, with a hat off. . . . You get the idea.

A GOING-HOME OUTFIT FOR BABY. This is the best part of packing your hospital bag. The outfit should be comfortable for Baby, and most important, it should be insanely cute. The cuter, the better! And you should have plenty of adorable outfits from which to choose thanks to your baby shower presents. If you don't know the sex of your baby ahead of time, you may opt to bring both a little boy and a little girl outfit, or you may decide to bring a neutral green, yellow, or white outfit. And keep in mind that even if you know ahead of time, those ultrasound technicians have been known to be wrong a time or two, and your newborn son probably won't appreciate the pictures of himself coming home from the hospital in a little pink dress with appliqué rosebuds, so you may want to have a backup.

Whatever you do, don't make the mistake of packing a gown to take Baby home in. You will have a hard time buckling Baby into their car seat if they're wearing a gown because you'll have to scrunch up the gown in order to get the strap to buckle between Baby's legs. Then her little legs will be cold. I learned this one the hard way. Thankfully, by the time I had my third baby, I knew and remembered this little tidbit. Yeah, I'm quite the expert.

The hospitals where I delivered all supplied a T-shirt and newborn hat, but they were really not all that fashionable, so you'll want to bring a cute T-shirt and hat of your own because this is the only time when you'll be able to dress your child without complaints.

Your infant can't talk back to you or take her outfit, throw it on the ground, and scream, "I don't wanna wear this! I don't like these clothes!" So you can pretty much dress your new baby in whatever you want. When they're toddlers, they'll insist on dressing themselves in combinations of colors and patterns so outrageous they'll make you dizzy. When your daughter is a teenager, you'll spend your time arguing over the appropriateness of her clothing. When your son is a teenager, you'll spend time explaining why he can't wear the same ratty old T-shirt five times a week. Enjoy your total control over what your baby wears now.

A PAIR OF SOCKS OR BABY BOOTIES. Babies' little footsies get cold easily and socks are essential even in the summer. Actually, babies can get even colder in the summer and warm climates because they'll spend time in air-conditioning. You need to put socks on Baby's feet so he can kick them off repeatedly. This is a good form of exercise for you—bending over and retrieving kicked-off socks. I've found little booties knit by a grandmother to be the best thing to put on Baby's feet. Grandmothers have the magical ability to make booties that stay on babies' feet. I don't know how. It's a closely guarded secret that I'm looking forward to learning when I have my own grandchildren.

A SEPARATE OUTFIT FOR BABY TO WEAR WHEN HAVING NEWBORN PICTURES TAKEN. This one's important because without a doubt, Baby will spit up on his cute clothes right before the photographer comes in the room. If she doesn't spit up on the clothes, her diaper will leak on the outfit. That's just the way it works with babies.

A RECEIVING BLANKET FOR BABY. You need this whether it's summer or winter, because you need something in which to receive your baby. Okay, honestly, I have no idea why it's called a receiving blanket. Are you supposed to use this blanket to receive the baby from somewhere? Where? Can the blanket only be used to receive your newborn? What if you give your baby to your mother to hold? Do you need a separate "handing off" blanket? I don't really get the name, but I know that newborns don't regulate their body temperature all that well and could get chilled from a cool breeze or air-conditioning. If it's winter, you'll want one of those toasty things that wrap around the car seat and keep baby in a snuggly cocoon of warmth. Whoever invented these wraps was a genius! I'm sure it was a mom who came up with this idea. Moms invent the *best* things for children! The wraps keep Baby nice and warm in transit, and when you get to your destination, all you do is simply unzip the wrap. Ta-da! Back in my day, we had to actually wake up our babies to get them unbundled from their snowsuits. You kids today have no idea how easy you have it! (Oops, I turned into my grandmother for a minute there. Sorry.)

SOME DIAPERS. My hospital provided diapers, as I think most hospitals do. However, you may want to pack a couple of your own just in case. My hospital also supplied size-one diapers, which were pretty big on my babies. I always packed a couple

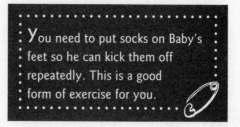

You need to put socks on Baby's feet so he can kick them off repeatedly. This is a good form of exercise for you.

newborn-sized diapers in my bag. If you intend to use cloth diapers, go ahead and pack a few of those; all hospitals I know supply only disposables.

A CAR SEAT. You definitely need to have an infant car seat for your baby. I'm not sure how it is in every state, but here in Illinois, they won't let you leave the hospital until you have Baby safely strapped in a car seat. You might want to practice this at home before you give birth. Strap a doll into the seat a couple times and install the seat into your car a few times so you're familiar with how it works. We must have spent a good hour and a half messing around with the car seat when Austin was born.

"You're not doing it right!"

"Well, since you know everything, why don't *you* do it!"

"Do you want our son to go flying out of the car? It's not tight enough!"

"I can't get it any tighter! Maybe we could just leave him at the hospital and come visit him now and then."

Much hormonal postpartum crying.

That's not really a good way to spend your first few moments as a family. Thankfully, car seats and newer vehicles now come equipped with the LATCH system, which makes car-seat installation infinitely easier than it was fifteen years ago. Still, to avoid unpleasant scenes, frustration, confusion, and embarrassment, practice putting in and taking out the seat before going to the hospital.

Infant car seats keep Baby safe while traveling by car, but they do so much more than that. They will serve as Baby's bed at times. When Baby falls asleep in a car seat, you can just leave him there, all safe and snuggly. When Baby is out of the car seat, the seat makes a handy holder for your purse, coat, diaper bag, or anything else you have lying around.

They can also double as a high chair. I remember using the car seat when I first started feeding my babies solid food because their high chairs still seemed so big for them. I would set the infant car seat on my kitchen table so my baby was nice and close, making it easy for feeding. It was especially wonderful being in such close vicinity when my baby sneezed out strained peaches and they splattered all over my face. Yep, the only thing more glamorous than being pregnant is being a mother.

A GOING-HOME OUTFIT FOR YOU. Now, I know you're sick and tired of maternity clothes and are just itching to get back into a pair of skinny jeans. I hate to burst your bubble, but it's not going to happen overnight. Even my tiny sister who looked like she'd never even been pregnant by the time her baby was three weeks old couldn't wear her jeans home from the hospital. You're going to need maternity clothes for your trip home from the hospital. I'm sorry, but it's the truth. Heck, some of us still needed maternity clothes when our babies started kindergarten. Ahem.

Anyway, pack something roomy and comfortable. You're going to be sore, and you're not going to want to wrestle with

> You're going to need maternity clothes for your trip home from the hospital. I'm sorry, but it's the truth.

snaps and buttons. Pack comfy sandals if it's summer and roomy tennis shoes or clogs if it's winter. You'll be amazed at how big your feet are by the time you leave the hospital. Have you ever seen an elephant's feet? Yours will be slightly larger after giving birth, and you'll appreciate comfy footwear.

You'll want to leave the thong at home and bring the big ole maternity underwear. These will be more comfortable and, believe me, you'll need that extra room to hold the mammoth-sized pads that you'll be wearing for the next few weeks.

Speaking of thongs, you will want to pack your own bag well ahead of time and I'll tell you why. It might seem silly to have a suitcase ready to go a couple months before you're due, but my friend Julie went into preterm labor well before she was due and didn't have a suitcase packed. Her husband had to pack a bag for her. If you don't want to open your bag to find sexy lingerie, the sparkly top you wore to a New Year's Eve party four years ago, a robe you haven't worn for years and is five sizes too small, high heels, and an obvious lack of shampoo, lotion, razor, and makeup, pack your own bag well ahead of time! Think about it, if your husband was at home packing a bag for you while you were in the hospital, what kinds of things would he put in it? Enough said.

SOME OF YOUR PADS. When I had my first two babies, the hospital provided me with those archaic pads of days gone by. You know, the kind that have to be belted on. Actually, you younger women probably have no idea what I'm talking about. In the *olden days*, sanitary pads didn't have tape that

stuck them to your un-
derwear. Nope, we had
to wear a nifty little
elastic belt that held
the ends of the pad in
place. The hospitals at

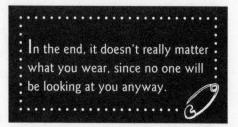

In the end, it doesn't really matter what you wear, since no one will be looking at you anyway.

which I delivered my last four babies had moved into this
century and had regular stick-on pads. Still, you might want
to bring a couple of your own just in case the ones they provide don't cut it for you.

A ROBE. You can leave the cute nightgowns at home. I know
that wearing something nice that fits you and doesn't have a
gaping opening in the back can boost your spirits, but if you
bring the nice nightie to the hospital, it will get messed up
with blood. It just will. Instead of bringing my own pajamas,
I wore the lovely hospital-issue gown with the ties in the
back. I did bring my own robe, however. If you think you
might have a steady stream of visitors, it can be a little disconcerting to sit there in that hospital gown with the gaping
hole in back and the giant nursing slits in front. Having your
own robe to cover up can help you maintain what little semblance of modesty you have left.

A COMFY NURSING BRA. If you plan on nursing your baby
(or if you're unsure whether you'll nurse or not), you'll
want to bring a nursing bra. This is essential. It seems like
I've spent half my life with a baby attached to my boobs.
Trust me on this one, you'll need a couple comfortable
nursing bras that fit well. The kind with fifteen hooks down

YOU'LL LOSE THE BABY WEIGHT

the back, enough underwire to suspend the Golden Gate Bridge, and four-inch-wide straps are best. Especially when you first start breastfeeding. You'll need all the help you can get. You don't want to mess around with trying to pull a regular bra down or take it off or whatever. Breastfeeding, opposed to what many people think, does not come automatically for most. It takes some practice and patience. Give yourself a break and get some comfy bras with clasps that open easily with one hand.

In the end, it doesn't really matter what you wear, since no one will be looking at you anyway. Just a couple days ago, you were the star, the center of attention. Everyone catered to you, the pregnant woman about to give birth. Now when you walk into a room carrying the baby, friends and relatives will push you aside without so much as a word so they can get a closer look at the new star—your sweet baby.

License and Registration, Please

Preeclampsia is a very serious problem that could lead to permanent damage. Thankfully, it can usually be controlled with bed rest, and/or medication. Signs of preeclampsia include high blood pressure, swelling of your hands and face, and protein in your urine.

When I was nine months pregnant with my fifth baby, the nurse found protein in my urine at a routine appointment. My blood pressure was just slightly elevated, but since I have fairly low blood pressure to begin with, it wasn't too bad. Because protein in the urine along with elevated blood pressure could be indicative of preeclampsia, the doctor was keeping a close eye on it.

He sent me home, told me to rest, and to return the following morning so he could recheck my blood pressure and urine. I'm not one to ignore doctor's orders, especially when the word *rest* is in them.

"Oh honey I'd love to make dinner, but the doctor told me to rest, and I always follow doctor's orders."

"I wish I could do some laundry, but I have to lie down. You know, doctor's orders."

Anyway, I went home, rested (well, as much as one can rest when they have four kids running around), and tried not to freak out that I was developing preeclampsia.

The following morning, I scooped some toilet water into my pee cup and headed back to the doctor's office. Because it was a Saturday and my husband was working, I had to drag all four kids with me. Once again, I was speeding just a teeny, tiny bit. As I was pulled over by an officer, I wondered why it seemed that I only got in trouble with the law when I was pregnant. As the police officer walked over to my car, I opened the window while my oldest kids shouted, "Mom's going to jail! Mom's going to jail!" The youngest was crying, and my middle son kept asking what was going on. "Why did you stop, Mommy? Who's that guy, Mommy? What's jail, Mommy?"

Trying to keep my cool, I turned to the kids. "I am NOT going to jail, now be quiet! Although, I bet it would be more peaceful in jail . . ." I trailed off.

The officer asked me for my license and registration. Registration? What's registration? Where's the registration? I'm sure I have registration somewhere. Where would it be? Oh yeah, the glove box! I bet it's in the glove box. I leaned over to grab my registration card, but I couldn't reach it because of my big, pregnant belly. I tried again. I rocked back a bit and then hoisted myself toward the passenger seat. No dice.

The officer just looked at me and asked, "Why are you in such a hurry?"

I told him the truth. "I'm nine months pregnant, and I'm on my way to my doctor's office. I have to get this pee there before they close," I said as I thrust my pee cup in his face. Oddly enough, this didn't seem to faze the officer.

"I might have preeclampsia and that's dangerous and he really needs this pee and my blood pressure's a little high and I've got all these kids with me and—" I stopped to breathe. (I tend to prattle on when I get nervous.)

He stared at me without an ounce of compassion and asked me for the registration once again. Darn! I should've just told him I was in labor. Of course, with my luck, he would have provided me with a police escort to the hospital, and then I would have had to fake labor. Not to mention the fact that I had four kids with me whom I'd have to entertain while I was in fake labor.

I got out of the car and waddled around to the passenger side so I could reach in and grab the card from the glove compartment. He took my license and registration, walked back to his squad car, and proceeded to write me out a ticket. Now, yes, I

> I leaned over to grab my registration card, but I couldn't reach it because of my big, pregnant belly.

was speeding and yes, I deserved a ticket, but I'm telling ya, a mom would've showed more understanding.

Anyway, after my little run-in with the law, my blood pressure was still elevated when I arrived at the office just before they closed. Fortunately, there was no longer any protein in my urine, and on subsequent checks, my blood pressure was always normal. So don't worry if you have a little protein in your urine one time. It doesn't necessarily mean anything. Your doctor will keep a close eye on you and make sure everything is all right. And if you happen to get pulled over for speeding, tell the police officer you're in labor.

You're STILL Pregnant???

You write your due date on the calendar and tell everyone you know (and probably some strangers on the subway or in the grocery store, too) when you expect your bundle of joy. I remember trying to figure out my due date the minute I got that positive pee stick. It was always so exciting to see the doctor take out his magical due-date calculator wheel at that first appointment. It's great to have your due date, or estimated date of delivery, as your doctor will probably call it. The important part of that is the word *estimated*. In other words, no one but God has a clue when you'll deliver. No one. It's merely an estimate. Pregnant women know this on an intellectual level, but it's so hard to remember that when you're counting down days until delivery. We mark off days on our calendars with big red *X*s until D-Day. But here's the thing, that "estimated date of delivery" can be off by two or more weeks in either direction.

With my first four babies, I ~~impatiently~~ eagerly awaited their arrival. My due dates, however, came and went and I was still without a baby. There's nothing quite so depressing as going beyond your due date. You've been waiting for nine months, for crying out loud. And now you have to wait *past* your due date! It's so not fair. It makes you want to march into your doctor's office, point to your calendar, and demand, "What's up with this? Do you see this day circled in red here? Well, that's when you said I'd have my baby. Look at me! I'm still pregnant! Where's my baby, Mister?!" I don't recommend actually doing this. Your doctor may suggest psychiatric help if you do.

I would tell you right now to look at your due date as more of a guide, an estimation, if you will, of when you'll deliver, but I know it won't matter. You'll still emblazon that date on your brain and believe heart and soul that it is THE day you'll deliver. It happens. I know this because still, to this day, I have a hard time remembering that Austin's birthday is November sixth. I always want to say it's the fourth, which in actuality was my due date. But try, at least, to keep in mind that you won't necessarily deliver on your actual due date. In fact, none of my friends delivered any of their babies on their due dates. Some were early and some were late, but none hit the exact day. I saw a study that said only four in a

No one but God has a clue when you'll deliver.

hundred women give birth on their actual due date. Really, given that information, we should probably be given something more like a "due fortnight" or a "due month." We'd be much more likely to deliver within the confines of an entire month than on one particular day.

If you end up going past your due date, never fear. It doesn't mean that you'll never deliver (even though it can feel like it at the time). Most women deliver by two weeks past their due date, or by forty-two weeks. If you go past your due date, there's certainly no reason for alarm, but your doctor will probably monitor you and your baby's health closely. This is a time when your doctor may order a non-stress test to just check on Baby and make sure he's still squirming around there and that his heart rate is fluctuating with his movement accordingly. As long as everything looks good, your doctor will likely ~~be really mean and make you wait~~ let you wait for labor to start on its own, naturally.

Biggest Fears About Labor and Delivery

1. *Being in labor forever.* I'm pretty sure this has never happened. Eventually, you'll give birth.

2. *Being unable to handle the pain.* That's what epidurals are for.

3. *Your water breaking in public.* Yeah, this could actually happen, but don't worry about it. People will probably just think you peed your pants.

4. *Being sent home in false labor.* If this happens, take solace in the fact that you're in good company.

5. *Never being able to lose the baby weight.* Yeah, well, I know nothing about this. Ahem.

6. *Being a bad parent, forgetting the baby, breaking the baby.* Relax. There is no such thing as a perfect parent. Besides, if you don't screw up your child a little bit, they'll have nothing to complain about as an adult.

7. *Fainting.* On the bright side, you won't feel the pain of labor if you pass out.

8. *Watching your husband faint.* If he faints, not only will he be unable to annoy you, but you'll have a fun story to tell for years to come.

9. *Losing control.* If you can't lose control in labor, when can you?

10. *Pooping on the table during delivery.* I got no help for you here.

CHAPTER 13

THE BIG DAY

Finally, after nine long months, delivery day is here! Yahoo! If this is your first baby, you're bound to be excited and nervous, scared and relieved at the same time. Although you've had time to read and study—and surely you've asked your doctor a thousand and one questions—you're still not sure what to expect. It can be really scary going into something as big as childbirth when you've never done it before and are just not sure what it will entail. I know, I remember being scared when I went to the hospital with Austin. Fear of the unknown can be pretty powerful. But keep this in mind, when it's all said and done, you'll have a brand-new baby and nothing beats that feeling. When you first get to hold your newborn baby and gaze into his or her eyes (or eyelids, if you opted to have a lot of pain medication and your baby's sleepy), you'll forget all about the pain and discomfort. It will just vanish in an instant. As you look at that precious, sweet face, you'll see just what an incredible miracle childbirth is. How can you have made something so amazing? How can this wonderful little soul have been growing inside you? It is nothing short of a miracle.

How Will You Know if You're in Labor?

When I was pregnant with my first baby, I was scared I'd go into labor and wouldn't realize it, and I'd end up giving birth to him on the bathroom floor. It's a common fear among first-time mothers. Believe me when I say that it will *never* happen. Don't believe me? Think of it this way: if two tons of bricks fell from the fifteenth story and landed on your head, do you think you'd notice it? Well, labor is slightly more painful than that. Believe me, you'll *know!*

You're much more likely to go to the hospital thinking you're in labor only to be sent home because you aren't quite ready yet. None of my friends missed the cues and got to the hospital too late with any of their kids. I mean, I guess it could happen theoretically, but I don't personally know anyone who has experienced this.

Although, if this isn't your first baby, getting to the hospital late is a distinct possibility since labor tends to progress more quickly in second and subsequent pregnancies. But on the bright side, you'll already know what labor feels like and should be able to plan accordingly to get to the hospital on time if this isn't your first baby. When I was pregnant with my fourth baby, I made it to the hospital in time, but my doctor didn't quite make it there. I was overdue with Lexi when my doctor, thinking that I was going to deliver a ten-pound baby, decided to induce labor. I went to the hospital, filled out the required four thousand forms, attempted to pee in a cup without getting any on my hand, and finally got hooked up to an IV of Pitocin. As the IV dripped into my vein, the contractions started. It wasn't long until I was in full-blown labor. After a while, a nurse checked my progress. "You're only dilated to four centimeters. You've got several hours to go," she stated confidently.

No sooner did she leave, than I got "that look" on my face. Having seen the look before, my husband recognized the fact that I was about to give birth. "Do you want me to get the doctor?" he asked.

I think he really expected me to answer him. But when you get to that point, there is no talking. If someone offered me a million dollars for doing nothing more than saying, "Yes," I'd have to pass. There is no talking when you're about to push out a baby. He repeated his question, but I was busy trying not to have my baby right there on the bed with no medical professionals in sight. Thankfully, Joe had been through this before and took my silence to mean, "Uh-oh, I better get the doctor." He ran out into the hall-way and searched for my doctor, who was nowhere in sight. He looked up and down the empty hallways for my nurse. He grabbed the first person he saw and dragged her into my room. Luckily, it happened to be one of my nurses and not a person visiting another patient!

This nurse came in, saw me pushing, and told me to stop. Um, hello? Stop? There is no stopping. There is no talking, and there is no stopping. There is no way on earth that you can physically stop pushing once that baby is ready to come out. It's a force of its own. She told me that I couldn't possibly be ready to push because I was only dilated to four. "You're not ready to push and you're going to do damage if you continue," Ms. Know-It-All Nurse haughtily informed me.

I shot her a look that was supposed to convey the following information: I've done this three times before! I KNOW what I'm doing. You're an idiot. Now back off or as soon as this baby comes out, I'm going to beat you with my IV pole!

She lifted my gown to check me and gasped when she saw the baby's head crowning. *I told you so!* echoed in my head. I wished I wasn't in the middle of having a baby, so I could grace her with a smug smile and an "I Told You So" song and dance.

So, there's my baby's head coming out. My bed hadn't been broken down. The cart with medical supplies for me hadn't been set up. The cart with medical supplies for the baby hadn't been set up. The baby warmer wasn't ready. The light hadn't been pulled down from its storage place up in the ceiling. And the nurse, who'd just happened to be passing by in the hallway, wasn't prepared for this at all. She quickly called out for help, and several people ran into my room. At this point, it didn't really matter that I had fourteen strangers

> In the middle of childbirth, all semblance of modesty goes right out the window.

looking at my hoo-ha. In the middle of childbirth, all semblance of modesty goes right out the window. There wasn't time to break down the bottom of my bed or don gloves, so she grabbed a piece of paper and caught Lexi with that.

I personally don't think I should've received a bill from my doctor for that one. Heck, I could've done that at home! Anyway, after Lexi's quickie birth, my doctors decided that perhaps I should have labor induced a couple days before my due date for any future pregnancies to help ensure that I would actually be at the hospital when I gave birth. That was music to my ears because, really, who would want to give birth in a car on the way to the hospital? Although come to think of it, it would make a great story, don't you think? Not that I'm willing to have any more kids just to get a great story. I'm just sayin' . . .

But for first-time moms, contractions, real contractions, are pretty darn painful. You're not likely to mistake real labor pain for indigestion. But how do you really know if you're in labor or if it's just more Braxton Hicks contractions? If it's false labor, the contractions will probably subside if you change your position and get up and walk around or lie down. With real labor, walking around will probably make your contractions intensify. With false labor, the contractions won't be regular and they won't increase in intensity or duration as time goes on. In real labor, the contractions will probably cause pain not only in your abdomen, but in your back as well. Along with the pain, if it's real labor, you'll begin to have a bloody discharge.

Before you get to this point, you'll want to talk to your doctor about when to call him. He'll probably tell you to call him if your water breaks. He'll probably also suggest a time frame in which to call him if you start having contractions. He might suggest, for example, that you call if your contractions are five minutes apart. Of course, if you think you're about to give birth in the middle of your living room, but your contractions are only nine minutes apart, go ahead and call your doctor. I promise he won't laugh at you if you're wrong and you aren't really that close to giving birth. Well, he might laugh at you behind your back, but I'm positive he won't laugh in your face. It's always better to err on the side of caution than to give birth in your car on the way to the hospital. Unless of course you're a writer, because that would make an awesome story!

Water Breaking

If you have a fear of your membranes rupturing in public, you're not alone. This was a huge fear of mine. I needn't have worried as my water never broke in public with any of my six pregnancies. Still, at the time I remember being scared that it would happen. I'm not sure why I was so scared. I mean, it's not like anyone would point and snicker if they saw a pregnant woman at the store, just dripping amniotic fluid. No, they would either offer to help or call an ambulance, or they'd turn tail and run the other way, but I'm pretty sure no one would laugh and whisper.

My friend Jen had her water break before she went into labor with three of her four pregnancies. One time it happened while she was having lunch with her mother at Baker's Square. Jen felt her water break as soon as they'd ordered their food. Since this wasn't her first baby, she knew that she'd better eat

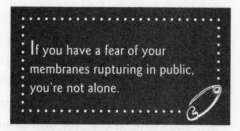

If you have a fear of your membranes rupturing in public, you're not alone.

now, or she'd be starved by the time she gave birth. So, despite the fact that her mother freaked out and announced the situation loudly enough for all the businessmen dining there to hear, Jen insisted they stay and eat before heading to the hospital. After hastily consuming her sandwich, she wrapped her coat around her waist and tried to make a nonchalant getaway without leaving a trail of amniotic fluid in her wake.

The only time my water broke before going into labor was with my first pregnancy, and as fate would have it, it broke in the shower! I planned that one well, no? When I was pregnant with my first baby, I anxiously, if a bit apprehensively, waited for the day that I'd go into labor. I'd read that when a baby is thirty-seven weeks, it's considered full term. So starting at thirty-seven weeks, I woke each day thinking it was the day I'd have my baby. Each day came and went. Thirty-eight weeks, thirty-nine weeks, forty weeks. My due date came and went, and let me tell you, that's depressing. A calendar with big red *X*s across each day leading up to your due date and beyond is a sad sight.

So the day after I was due, I slept in late (I could do that back then, I didn't have any kids yet). I got up and took a shower around noon. As I was showering, I felt warm water dripping down my legs. It seemed a little strange. I wasn't sure if it was water from the shower or if I was peeing (hey, I was nine months pregnant, and my bladder control wasn't what it used to be), or if my water had broken. I quickly turned off the shower to see if it stopped. Nope, I still had the warm water trickling down my legs. I got out, dried off, and came to the conclusion that my water had broken. I was thrilled that I was finally going to have a baby! Then I realized—oh my gosh! I'm going to have a baby!—and promptly started hyperventilating. But beyond the excitement and nervousness was a huge sense of relief. My water hadn't broken in public! And I didn't have to worry about going into labor and not recognizing the fact that I was having contractions.

Induction

After my water broke in the shower, I called my doctor, who told me to take my time but head to the hospital soon. After arriving at the hospital, filling out admission forms, peeing in a cup, and changing into a gown, the nurses asked me, "Are you having contractions now?"

I answered confidently, "Yes! Well, I think I am. I'm not sure. Maybe? I think I'm having little contractions. They don't really hurt. I don't know."

The nurses exchanged looks with each other that said, "Oh great. She's one of *those* patients." They hooked me up to a monitor which told them that no, I was definitely not having any contractions yet. The nurse shook her head at my stupidity, unhooked the monitor, and told me to walk around. After several hours, I still wasn't having contractions, so my doctor opted to start a Pitocin drip to get things started since it had been several hours since my water had broken.

Some women don't like being induced and prefer to let nature take its course in its own sweet time. Discuss this with your practitioner if this is your preference. Your doctor may be able to hold off inducing labor as long as both you and Baby appear to be doing well. Other times, you won't have much of a say in it. If it looks like your placenta is no longer functioning well and your baby isn't thriving, you may need to have labor induced. If, like me, your membranes break and labor doesn't start on its own, your doctor will probably induce you to cut down the chances of infection. Your doctor may also opt to induce if your baby is overdue or if it looks like your baby will be very large and difficult to deliver. If you have diabetes or preeclampsia and your baby's health is in danger, your doctor may induce labor as well. And, of course, he might schedule an induction if he thinks you might deliver in the middle of his Super Bowl party, for example.

I personally liked having labor induced. For a variety of reasons, I had labor induced or augmented with all six of my babies. Doctors generally induce labor with the drug Pitocin. This is administered through an IV drip. Nurses can control how much you get by adjusting the IV pump. They start out with a little bit and continue to turn it up every few minutes until you're ~~screaming in pain~~ in active labor. I liked it because although contractions were intense, they were regular and labor moved along fairly quickly. My attitude was, "Okay, I'm here. Let's have this baby already and make it speedy!"

Some of my friends disagree with me. They say that contractions are milder with naturally occurring labor. They didn't like the sudden onset of labor that Pitocin can bring on. They preferred to have their contractions slowly progress. I think they're nuts, but I've always been an impatient kind of girl.

Monitoring

If you give birth in a hospital or medical facility, you'll probably have some sort of fetal monitoring. I had monitors strapped to me for each of my labors and deliveries. My friends and I all had the same kind of monitors for each of our babies. They looked like two small plastic hockey pucks and they were set on our abdomens and held in place by ginormous elastic bands. These monitors measure Baby's heartbeat in relation to your contractions. Usually the readings are displayed on a screen in your room and, if you're in a high-tech hospital, also on a screen at the nurses' station, which allows your nurse to keep tabs on you without having to come into your room every few minutes. It will be printed out on a never-ending piece of paper as well. On the paper, you'll see two lines. One measures Baby's heart rate. The other line measures contractions. You'll see little "mountains" in the line every time you have a contraction. As the contraction subsides, the line dips back down to the baseline.

The reason doctors put fetal monitors on you is so your husband can look at the printout and say helpful stuff like, "Oh, you're having another contraction right now," just in case you aren't aware of the horrendous pain in your abdomen. Then he can say stuff like, "Oh, that didn't look like a bad one," when his expertly trained eye decides the line didn't rise enough to make it a "bad" contraction. In such cases, by the way, it is completely acceptable to hit your spouse over the head with a bedpan.

Give Me Drugs

Yes, labor hurts. In Genesis 3:16, we read: "To the woman he said, 'I will greatly increase your pains in childbearing; with pain you will give birth to children.'" I knew there was a reason I hated snakes.

But it doesn't have to be the most horrific pain you've ever felt in your life. There are plenty of pain medications available for use in labor. I'm just going to concentrate on the three different ones that I have experience with: epidurals, the shot cocktail, and nothing but prayer. Most of my friends order an epidural the minute they get that little pink line on an over-the-counter pregnancy test. I have a couple friends who are die-hard "natural childbirth" supporters. I fall somewhere in between. I think it's great if you can get through childbirth without drugs, but it's more important to get through labor and delivery without falling apart at the seams, and if pain medication is what you need to make that happen, then by all means, that's what you should have.

I really want to stress how important it is to keep an open mind on this, though. You might want to draw up a birthing plan and have an idea of how you'd like things to go, so you can look back at it later and laugh about how clueless you were, and how nothing went as you planned. When I was pregnant with my first baby, I was adamant about not taking any kind of pain relief. I was sure I could get through labor and delivery just fine on my own and that women who had to have epidurals were just big sissy babies. You know, because I was completely stupid. I think I was in labor for five minutes before yelling, "I need something for this terrible, unbearable pain! Oh for crying out loud, woman, get over here with some drugs NOW!"

A nurse came in and gave me a shot of something "to take the edge off." *Take the edge off* is a term nurses use that means the same as, "Do nothing at all for your pain." These magical cocktails work by basically making you too loopy and tired to care that you're still in pain. Seriously, some of the drugs/combinations of drugs that your doctor may use can actually make you doze off between contractions. With most of my labors, this was all I needed to get through the pain until it was time to push. These medications will take the edge off your labor pain, but will not entirely get rid of it. For some women, this is great middle ground between an epidural and nothing at all. They feel that they still get to fully experience

> I was sure I could get through labor and delivery just fine on my own—you know, because I was completely stupid.

labor without being completely numb and without being in excruciating pain.

Ask your doctor the names of the pain relievers he uses in labor so you can ask for them by name in a year or two, when your baby is coloring in permanent marker on your new coffee table, or shaving the dog, and you just need a little something to help you not lose control and yell at your child in five different languages. Different doctors use different drugs and/or combinations of drugs to help control labor pain. And keep in mind that these are not without drawbacks. Just as they make you feel loopy and tired, they can have the same effect on your baby. If you've taken some sort of pain-relieving medication in labor, your baby can be born very sleepy and out of it. Again, remember the name of the drugs he uses because they could also come in handy when that same baby is two and is lying down on the floor in the middle of the grocery store, screaming because he wants a candy bar NOW. Not that I would ever recommend drugging your child or anything.

Shortly after I had my magical cocktail shot while I was in labor with Austin, I found myself calling the nurse back. "About that shot . . . do you have any more? Please! Actually, skip the stupid shot and give me the epidural! This is for the birds! No human on earth could take this kind of pain!" Hey, it was my first delivery. I didn't know what to expect. It was an especially painful labor. I was young. Okay, okay, I was a big sissy baby. I didn't know how much more pain I could take. When I ~~begged~~ asked for the epidural, I thought I might be in labor for another year and a half, and I knew I couldn't take the pain that much longer. I think that's the worst thing about labor pain—not knowing how long it will last. If someone had told me I'd be in pain for only another half an hour, I probably could've sucked it up and dealt with it, knowing the end was in sight, but unfortunately no one can tell you just how long your labor will last.

The anesthesiologist came in and prepared to give me the epidural. Epidurals are given by anesthesiologists, who like to torture women. They will have you sit up and then lean forward so your spine is nice and curved. No big deal, right? Until you have a contraction and you nearly fall off the bed, that is. It is SO hard to sit there nice and still while he's poking around at your back, especially when you're having horrible two-minute-long contractions.

As you sit there, trying to remember how to breathe and concentrating on not falling off the side of the bed, the anesthesiologist will jab you in the back with a twelve-foot needle, and the whole time you'll be thinking, *He's sticking a big fat needle in my back! What if I have a contraction that causes me to fall over in pain? My sudden movement will make him miss and hit my spinal cord and I'll never be able to walk again!* As he administers the medication, you're supposed to feel relief. According to my friends, after their epidurals took effect (which was almost immediately), they didn't feel any pain from their contractions at all. The only way they knew they were having a contraction was by looking at the monitor. This was not the case with me. I continued to feel each and every contraction just as strongly as before my epidural. As I started to complain to the nurse, my baby's heart rate dropped. The nurses all rushed in, flipped me to my left side, and put an oxygen mask on me.

I, being a calm rational person, took all this in stride. "Oh my gosh! What's wrong?! What's wrong? Is my baby okay? Oh my

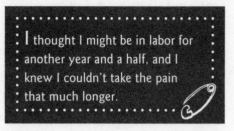

I thought I might be in labor for another year and a half, and I knew I couldn't take the pain that much longer.

gosh! What's going on?!" I believe were my exact words. As it turns out, my baby's heart rate went back up with me lying on my left side and breathing extra oxygen. He was fine and was born shortly afterward. I, on the other hand, never experienced any pain relief from that epidural. In fact, it seems the epidural all went to my left leg instead of my abdominal area. My leg was numb for the rest of the day, and I couldn't get up to walk until several hours later.

This is not the usual reaction. Epidurals don't generally work like that. In fact, I'm the only person I know who had that experience. Most of my friends swear by epidurals and send their anesthesiologists Valentine's Day cards every year, professing their undying love and gratitude.

My nurse convinced me to try an epidural again when I was pregnant with Jackson, as it was a very long labor. I agreed. The anesthesiologist was barely out the door from giving me the epidural when I pushed Jackson out. I called him back, "Um, I don't think this counts. Can you just not give me a bill for this since technically, I delivered my baby before the epidural took effect?" That was the last time I tried an epidural.

The other way I've dealt with pain is by taking no pain medication and simply concentrating on not feeling pain. Okay, I know, I know, that sounds ridiculous even to me.

Almost as silly as breathing in order not to feel pain. Honestly though, with most of my labors and deliveries, I simply concentrated on something, anything, to kind of forget about the pain. I'd sing song lyrics in my head when a contraction was going on. To this day, when I hear the soundtrack from *Joseph and the Amazing Technicolor Dreamcoat,* I think about being in labor with Clayton. I'd picture my other kids' faces during the pain. I'd stare at a ceiling tile and try to count how many dots were on it. (One hundred twenty-three, in case you're interested.) I mostly just zoned out and went into my own mind every time I had a contraction.

I know it sounds a little goofy, but it worked for me. Of course, I had to smack my husband a couple times for trying to talk to me while I was concentrating. I didn't want to talk. I didn't want him to touch me or give me ice chips or anything. I just wanted to be left alone so I could go into my own little pain-free world. Thankfully, my nurses got this and would leave me alone until the contraction passed before asking me questions or taking vitals.

Whatever method you think you'd like to try while in labor, please keep an open mind. Although you might not want to take pain medication now, you may find yourself needing something to get through those last couple hours of labor. Conversely, although you may think you're going to need an extra-strength epidural the minute you walk in the hospital

> Of course, I had to smack my husband a couple times for trying to talk to me while I was concentrating.

doors, you might find yourself getting by just fine without any pain medication. Ask your doctor and learn about the different methods of pain relief he uses, and then play it by ear and see how you feel.

The Phases of Labor

Doctors divide childbirth into three stages: labor, pushing and delivery, and finally delivery of the placenta. Labor is further divided into phases ~~just to make it more confusing for you~~. I'll explain a little about those phases of labor.

FIRST PHASE: During the first phase of labor, the cervix opens to three centimeters. That's a good start, but take out a ruler and measure off three centimeters. See what I mean? No baby is coming out of an opening that size. You could barely squeeze a Polly Pocket out of that opening, let alone a seven-pound baby.

For most of my friends, this first stage of labor passed without their even realizing it. They were dilated to three before they ever felt a labor pain. Sometimes those Braxton Hicks contractions actually do work to get labor started. I, on the other hand, never dilated so much as a millimeter before I went into labor. In fact, this was always the longest stage of labor for me. It generally took several hours to get to this point. I'm just lucky that way, I guess.

If this phase hasn't passed unnoticed by you, and you're having actual, painful contractions, you'll probably still be able to talk and walk through the contractions until the end of this phase. Labor at this point feels kind of like really bad menstrual cramps. Contractions last about thirty to forty-five seconds and come every five to twenty minutes during this phase. You may think to yourself, *This isn't so bad. Labor doesn't really hurt. I can handle this!* Labor generally starts off slowly so we have time to get acclimated to the ~~horrific, hellish, horrendous~~ pain yet to come. You'll probably have a little bloody show and possibly even diarrhea (which is a good thing, because if you empty your bowels now, you won't have to worry about pooping during delivery). Have I mentioned how this was my greatest fear going into labor and delivery? Well, let me tell you again. I was petrified of pooping while giving birth!

Although your nurses will offer you a gourmet snack of ice chips, you may want to eat a little something now, before you head to the hospital. You don't want to eat a thirty-two-ounce slab of prime rib with all the fixings because women in labor often throw up. (I know, I know, will the list of awful symptoms never end?) Eat something that you won't mind coming back up on you. Some soup, toast, or a banana would make a great, light snack to help hold you over without sitting like a rock in your stomach.

Let your husband, or whoever is going to the hospital with you, know you're in labor, but don't stress out and head to the hospital quite yet. Unless your husband is likely to react like the stereotypical dad-to-be from television shows of old, that is. If you're afraid he'll start babbling incoherently, grab his keys, head out the door in nothing but his underwear, and leave skid marks as he screeches down your driveway only to realize he forgot your suitcase, come back inside, grab your bag, screech down the driveway again, real-ize he forgot you, and come back inside, you might want to hold off

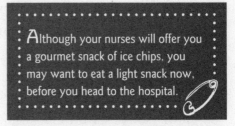

Although your nurses will offer you a gourmet snack of ice chips, you may want to eat a light snack now, before you head to the hospital.

telling him you're in labor until you're a little further along. Go about your regular routine and finish anything you need to do around your house. Call everyone you know, and maybe make some random calls to strangers as well, and tell them you're in labor. If it's the middle of the night, most pregnancy books will tell you to go back to sleep. Clearly, they've never gone into labor in the middle of the night. You and I both know you'll be too excited to sleep. I sug-gest you pop in a movie to help keep your mind off your im-pending delivery and relax while you can.

SECOND PHASE: During this phase, your cervix will dilate to seven centimeters and new meaning will be given to the word *pain*. This phase of labor is generally shorter than the first phase. It usually lasts a couple hours. Contractions will last about forty to sixty seconds and come every three to four minutes now. Use the time between contractions to rest—you'll need all the energy you can muster for the next phase. Contractions will start to hurt in the way that drop-ping a sledgehammer on your foot hurts. Or like diving off the high dive into an empty pool hurts. Or like being dragged behind a truck going ninety miles an hour hurts. Or like listening to your kids fight over something really im-portant like a piece of gum hurts.

It will take all your concentration to get through these contractions, and you may need medication for pain now. Your husband will become super-annoying at this point even if he's ordinarily the best guy in the world. You might find yourself irritated when he talks, touches you, breathes, and just exists in the same room. You'll probably have more bloody show and some pain in your back, as well as your abdomen.

If your membranes haven't already broken on their own, your doctor will likely rupture them at some point during this phase of labor. The first time this happened to me, my doctor prefaced the procedure with the requisite "This won't hurt a bit" before pulling out a tool that looked like a giant crochet hook. I eyed the medieval weapon, looked at my doctor with raised eyebrow, then fastened my gaze back on the torture device. *Yeah,* I thought, *that doesn't look like it'll hurt,* as I leapt from the bed and took off running down the hall, my gown flapping in the breeze. Those poor pregnant women and their husbands who were walking up and down the halls at that moment got more than they ever wanted to see.

Really, it doesn't hurt much, if at all, when the doctor breaks your membranes. Feeling the gush of warm fluid drenching you and your bed is more disconcerting than anything. Your nurses will put several absorbent layers under you before your doctor breaks your water, and they'll discard it and clean you up afterward, but for those few moments when you're lying in a pool of wetness, it's icky. That's the most accurate word I can come up with— icky.

As soon as your bag of waters is broken, you'll experience a new intensity to your labor. With your water broken, Baby can slide down farther in the birth canal and put ~~you through gut wrenching, searing, agonizing, blinding pain~~ considerable pressure on your cervix.

Change positions now and then. It usually helps move things along when you switch which side you're lying on. You'll probably need someone to help hoist up your big belly and all the monitors and wires if you turn over or get up to use the bathroom or walk around. You may be able to walk around at the beginning of this phase, but you probably won't want to be up and around toward the end of it. Go to the bathroom when you need to, and don't worry about accidentally giving birth to your baby while you're on the toilet, not that I ever worried about that or anything. Just sayin' . . .

You may find it soothing for your husband to rub your back or put cool washcloths on your forehead here. You might like it if he holds your hand or brushes your hair back from your face. You may feel relaxed if he plays music for you or massages your legs. Then again, you might find it soothing if he just shuts up and stays out of your line of sight. Let him know what you need from him, and do not expect him to have a clue on his own.

THIRD PHASE: During the third phase, your cervix will dilate from seven all the way to ten. You may recall how your childbirth educator told you to envision your cervix as a flower gently opening. At this point, when I envisioned a flower opening, it's wasn't a dainty rosebud. It was the plant from the Little Shop of Horrors, and it swallowed the instructor whole. *That'll serve her right for telling me I won't feel any pain if I just breathe! Humph!*

This is the most intense phase of labor, but thankfully, it's also the shortest. In four of my six deliveries, it lasted only a couple minutes. I think a more general average, however, is under an hour.

During this phase, you will just about lose it. You will begin to think, *I can't do this!* Usually, about the time you start wishing you could travel back in time nine months and tell your husband you have a headache, you'll be ready to push. During this phase, many women throw up. It's common. You won't waste time worrying about it, though, because you'll be too busy crying like a baby at the pain you're in. I'm pretty sure this is the phase Carol Burnett was thinking about when she described labor pain—"Take your bottom lip and pull it over your head."

And it's not just pain at this point. Many women start shaking uncontrollably. I always knew when it was about time for me to push because I couldn't stop shaking. I wasn't cold; I just couldn't stop shaking. And this is no ordinary shaking like when you're chilled. Oh no, this is a whole-body experience where every muscle in your entire being convulses and you shake until you get achy.

You will have a lot of bloody show, and you'll feel a ton of pressure. I was told that it will feel like you have to poop as you near the end of your labor. I agree. You know, if you were to have a seven-pound poop, that is. When the need to push hit me, I always started grunting involuntarily. Pretty much everything about this phase of labor is involuntary.

You shake, you throw up, you have almost unbearable pain, and you grunt and start pushing automatically without any conscious thought.

During this phase of labor, you can no longer rest between contractions because they're pretty much on top of one another and the overwhelming need to bear down doesn't make resting a possibility. Contractions last sixty to ninety seconds (which is the same thing as two hours) with no break in between. If he hasn't already, your husband (and possibly your doctor and nurses as well) will probably irritate you to no end. Try to tune them out and concentrate on getting your baby out.

As you near the end of this phase, you may notice you suddenly have more people in your room. Instead of poking his head in the door every couple hours, your doctor may start hanging out in your room now. You'll probably have two or three nurses appear. At least one will care for you and another one will care for Baby once he or she makes his or her grand entrance. If you're lucky, you may have some medical students, interns, a person from food service carrying a tray to your room by mistake just to taunt you, a janitor who thinks she has to mop the floor right now for some reason, and perhaps a maintenance guy. That happened to me when I was in labor with Austin. A maintenance guy came in to fix the thermostat. You might think that would be terribly embarrassing, but when you feel like your guts are being turned inside out, I promise you won't care if the entire defensive line of the Chicago Bears, the Vienna Boys' Choir, and Captain Jack Sparrow waltz into your room.

They'll take the bottom part of your bed off and pull out some stirrups. You'll be in too much pain to move, but the staff will maneuver your big body into position and get your feet in the stirrups. A huge light will appear from the ceiling and a baby warmer will be set up. You may or may not notice these things happening since you'll be delirious with pain.

Special Delivery

When you finally hear the words "It's time to push," you'll experience a sense of relief coupled with a new fear. *I'm almost there! I'm going to meet my baby in a few minutes! But how on earth am I going to squeeze a baby out of me?* When it's time to push, your nurses will grab your legs and push them up until your feet touch your ears. The reason they fold you into a pretzel is to ~~make sure your legs hurt as much as your entire midsection~~ make it a little easier to push out your baby. When you have a contraction, your nurses will tell you to push while they count to four thousand. I don't know why they count. Somewhere along the line, someone came up with the great idea of counting as you push. I personally have a problem with people counting as I push. It's just too reminiscent of those horrid exercise tapes where a skinny girl who hasn't broken a sweat, with her face made up and not a hair out of place, tells you something stupid like, "You can do it! Just ten more. One, two, three, four, five . . . ." I just want to yell back, "Shut up! This hurts! Easy for you to sit there and tell me only ten more!" Maybe it wouldn't be so bad if your nurse talked like the Count from Sesame Street. "One! One contraction! Ha-ha-ha-ha! Two! Two contractions! Ha-ha-ha-ha!" Then again, maybe not.

Now, I know it won't seem natural to push with all your might. I mean, delivery feels much like having a bowel movement, and that's just not something we want to do in front of a roomful of strangers. It will seem awkward to grunt and push hard. We naturally want to be more ladylike and do small, dainty little pushes. Fight the urge to be dainty! Push with all your strength. Unless you want to be there pushing for hours, give it all you've got. Don't let your fear of pooping keep you from pushing. I promise you, if you poop, no one will care and you won't even feel it because of the searing pain down there.

Right before your baby comes out, your doctor may perform an episiotomy. *Episiotomy* is the medical term for "Oh my gosh, did you just CUT me down there???" Women are extremely stretchy, and openings that are usually very small can stretch enough to let an eight-pound baby pass through. It's amazing, really. That said, sometimes it's necessary for a doctor to help things along. An episiotomy is a procedure wherein the doctor takes a pair of scissors and cuts you down there! Yeah, I know it sounds like the most evil thing ever, but there's a good reason why they do it. My first obstetrician performed episiotomies routinely with the reasoning that a straight incision heals better than a big jagged tear. I had episiotomies with my first three babies. My fourth baby was born before the doctor even got to my room, so needless to say,

I didn't have my perineum cut to enlarge the vaginal opening in order to allow for the passage of Baby's head. Instead, I tore. I've got to say, it was a much easier and much less painful recovery with that small tear than it was when I had the episiotomies.

Some nice midwives say this procedure isn't necessary. They'll try techniques like massaging the perineal area, warm compresses, and enlisting a more upright position for giving birth. They state that episiotomies aren't really necessary and that if the perineum doesn't stretch enough on its own, a small tear would be better than a surgical incision.

Now, I have some friends who did not get episiotomies, and they really wish they had. I have a couple friends who tore badly and needed extensive repair. They had miserable recoveries. For them, it would've been better if the doctor had just pulled out his handy scissors. I don't really think there's a right or wrong answer to the question, *To cut or not to cut?* However, there is a very definite answer to the question, *Will it hurt?* and that is a resounding *Yes!*

Whether you have an episiotomy or not, as your baby's head crowns, you'll experience a burning sensation like none you've ever felt. But the good news is that all pain will completely disappear the second your baby slides out. I don't know how this works, but it does. Ask anyone who's had a baby, and she'll tell you the same. The pain vanishes. Poof! It's gone, just like that!

Cesarean Sections

I don't have any experience with C-sections. I never needed one with any of my deliveries. Still, whether you're planning on having a cesarean birth or not, every woman should be prepared for the possibility just in case—because you just never know. Ask your doctor about his procedures for a cesarean delivery, and pay attention when they cover C-sections in your childbirth class.

For a variety of reasons (such as preeclampsia, diabetes, and a previous C-section, among others), a C-section may be scheduled before you go into labor. In these cases, you can prepare yourself. And as long as Baby and Mom are doing well and time isn't a factor, your husband should be able to be in the operating room with you when your baby is born. Also, you should be able to be awake for the procedure and see your baby right after she's born. Ask your doctor about his rules for how soon you can hold and nurse your baby after a cesarean delivery.

If an emergency arises and time is of the essence, you may have to have an emergency C-section, in which case, you might be put out with general anesthesia to ensure that the delivery of your baby is the quickest and safest for both of you.

According to my friends who had C-sections, the biggest issue they faced, aside from a more difficult recovery and abdominal soreness for weeks, was the feeling of failure and disappointment they experienced. Really, there is no need to feel like a failure because your baby was taken out surgically instead of pushed out by you. You are a mother and have

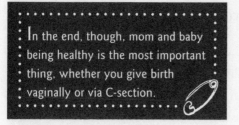

In the end, though, mom and baby being healthy is the most important thing, whether you give birth vaginally or via C-section.

endured an incredible experience no matter how your baby is born. Although no woman is a failure if she needs a C-section, I can understand why some women have feelings like this. After all, you look forward to labor and delivery throughout your pregnancy. You fantasize about it for months. And for most of us, those fantasies don't include a sterile environment and a surgical incision. It's tough when labor doesn't happen the way we think it is *supposed* to happen.

In the end, though, mom and baby being healthy is the most important thing, and whether you give birth vaginally or via C-section, the end result is a beautiful new baby—and that's always good. Besides, when your child gets old enough to ask the uncomfortable question "How did I get out of your tummy, Mommy?" you can give the easy answer of "The doctor lifted you out of my tummy."

For Fathers: What NOT to Do in the Delivery Room

I mentioned that fathers shouldn't comment on your level of pain based on the monitor's rise and fall of your contractions. My friends begged me to go a step further, however, and talk about some other things that dads-to-be do in the delivery room that can really tick off moms-to-be. So, Dads, this section is for you. I went online and asked my friends for their number one piece of advice for expectant fathers on things they should and shouldn't do so they could avoid getting a bedpan thrown at their head. I had e-mails with comments come in faster than I could read them! This is one subject we women feel very strongly about.

So here, in no particular order, is your best advice to expectant fathers:

Do not touch your wife unless she asks you to: Do not rub your wife's head. Do not touch her arm. Do not massage her hands. Do not assume she wants a back rub. In fact, don't touch her in any way, shape, or form unless she asks you to rub her back or hold her hand or brush her hair back. Do not get all offended if you follow this advice and your wife gets mad that you didn't automatically know to rub her back without her asking you. We're in serious pain. We can't be expected to be logical when in labor.

Do not touch the remote control. I don't care if the stinkin' Super Bowl is on. You should be watching your precious wife, not the TV. Period. Watching sports, stupid shows, or just flipping through channels is grounds for divorce. If your wife wants to watch TV, you need to watch whatever she wants to watch. If she doesn't, you need to make sure you don't touch the remote control. And don't complain about it either.

Do not eat anything in front of your wife. Do not bring food into the delivery room. Do not talk about what you're going to eat for lunch or dinner or whatever. She hasn't had anything but stupid ice chips to eat, and she's having the workout of her life. If she can make it without food while giving birth, you can surely go a few hours without food while just sitting there.

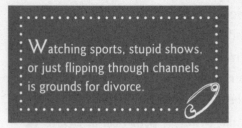

Watching sports, stupid shows, or just flipping through channels is grounds for divorce.

If it's okay with your wife, leave the room to eat and make sure you don't eat anything with onions or garlic, or she will probably kick you in the shins when you return to the room and breathe near her face.

Do not sleep. I don't care if you've been awake for twenty hours. Guess what? So has your wife! And she's in too much pain to sleep. Stay awake and keep her company! If you fall asleep and start snoring, your wife has every right to stab you with a hypodermic needle.

Do not comment on your wife's pain. Do not say, "It's okay. You're okay." Do not ask, "Is it really that bad? Does it really hurt that much? It doesn't seem that bad." Don't make comments about the level of pain you think your wife is or isn't experiencing. Don't compare her pain to your surgery, stitches, or broken bones. You have no idea what it's like. You've never given birth. You don't know. Period.

Don't ask your wife questions and look at her expectantly for an answer while she's having a contraction. In fact, don't talk to your wife at all unless you're answering her question. I'm sorry, but it's just a fact. Listening to a husband's stupid questions and inane babbling can be very irritating to a woman in labor. You might be the sweetest guy on earth and you may only be interested in your wife's well-being, but in all honesty, we just don't want to hear you talk while we're in labor. It takes all our concentration to get through a contraction, and conversation is just annoying while we're dealing with the pain.

Do not talk on the phone to your buddies or your mother or anyone, unless your wife has specifically asked you to make or take a phone call for her. Saying something like, "I can't wait 'til this is over" or "I'm so tired/hungry/bored" is also grounds for divorce. You have the easy job here. There is no complaining allowed from you.

Do not downplay her pain. As I stated before, do not look at the fetal monitor and tell your wife when she is having a contraction. She KNOWS when she's having a contraction! Do not look at the monitor and say, "Oh that's not a bad one." Based on the monitor, you have no idea if it was a "bad one"! Also, do not argue with your wife if she says she's having a contraction no matter what the fetal monitor looks like. Don't argue with her if she says she has to push or she's in pain. Pretty much, don't argue with her at all.

Do not announce that more than just the baby came out. We do not need to know that we just pooped while giving birth. Poop happens. We can't even feel that with all the pain we're in, and we'd prefer to remain blissfully ignorant, so don't bring it up!

Do not make any sexual innuendos. Do not ask, while smirking, "So, you ready to have another one?" *Wink wink.* Believe me, if you do, it will be a looooong time before that's even a possibility! *Wink wink.* Do not ask the doctor to "put in an extra stitch down there, if you know what I mean." If you do, there's a good chance you'll be sleeping in the garage for the next year.

Do not say anything negative about the baby. Do not look at your precious newborn baby that you've waited nine months to see and say, "Ewww, he/she looks so slimy/

bloody/yucky!" This is your baby you're talking about here! The only way to describe him or her is "beautiful"!

Honestly, just be there for your wife. Be there for her when she wants something. Remember that she has to stay awake. She has to go without eating. And she's in a lot of pain. She's going through this to bring your baby into this world. Show her how much you appreciate her by just being there for her. Just because she may have told you before she went into labor that she wants you to rub her back doesn't mean she still wants that now that she's in pain. Keep in mind that even though she may be acting irrationally right now, she loves you. She may not show it while she's in labor, but you still can. She'll be back to herself soon, and she'll love and appreciate you more than ever if you're just considerate of her feelings while she's in labor. And if you end up getting a bedpan thrown at you, at least there will be plenty of nurses around to attend to your bruises.

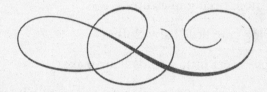

Best Things About Having a Baby

. . . .

1. Tax deduction

2. You're no longer pregnant!

3. That sweet baby smell

4. You can once again reach to shave your legs.

5. No more peeing in a cup

6. Buying cute little baby clothes

7. Those sweet little sounds Baby makes

8. No more strangers coming up and patting your belly (at least, I hope not!)

9. Someone to pass your chores on to in the future

10. Having someone to unconditionally love for the rest of your life

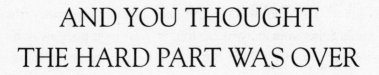

CHAPTER 14

AND YOU THOUGHT
THE HARD PART WAS OVER

Y ou've waited nine months for your baby. You've endured all the discomforts of pregnancy for nine whole months. You've made it through labor and delivery like a trooper and your payoff is the gift of a precious little soul entrusted to your care. You now have a sweet-smelling little miracle—a combination of your husband and you to love and shower with affection. So, now what? Well, even though the main event is over, you're not done with the whole experience yet. In fact, technically, you'll never be done. Once you're a mother, you're always a mother, and this is your new life forever.

But right after birth, you enter the postpartum period, and it's worth talking about some of the things that will be happening to you throughout the weeks following the delivery of your baby.

The Best Way to Lose Ten Pounds

The greatest thing about delivery is that you're no longer pregnant. Okay, actually the greatest thing is, of course, that you now have a precious, beautiful baby. But running a close second is the fact that you're no longer pregnant— hooray! The pain of labor, the discomfort of pregnancy, the feeling that your body is no longer your own goes away *the instant* your baby slides out. You'll be amazed at the transition. Baby comes out—you can breathe. Just like that. Now if only all the extra weight came off so easily!

Honestly, I felt such an incredible relief after I pushed my babies out, I didn't even notice the delivery of the placenta or the doctor sewing up my episiotomy. Okay, well maybe I "noticed" it, but I was feeling too good to care about it.

Speaking of the placenta, you may want to avert your eyes if you're squeamish. When I first saw the placenta, I made a comment about it looking like cranberry sauce. Let me tell ya, Thanksgiving hasn't been the same since. You might want to also warn your husband not to shout out, "Ew, it looks like liver!" Instead, focus on the fact that this is what has been nourishing your bundle of joy for the past several months. And look the other way.

The good thing about episiotomy repair is that you're usually still fairly numb down there so the pain isn't too horrible. Oh, who am I kidding? Getting stitched up stinks. It hurts. My doctor warned me, "This may sting a little," as she stitched me up. Just so you know, *sting a little* is the medical term for "hurt like a red-hot branding iron!" And while the doctor is sticking a NEEDLE in quite possibly the most sensitive area on your entire body, you're lying there just itching for him to finish up so you can hold your new baby! My friend Denise had tears that took her doctor a long time to repair. As he was stitching away, she told him, "Make sure you sew me up in a nice, straight line." He responded with, "I'm embroidering my initials on you." Being a quick thinker, my friend Denise laughed and said, "Well, I guess it's a good thing we have the same initials then!"

After being stitched up, your nurses will clean you up. While all this is going on, other nurses will be taking care of your baby. They'll place him under warming lights and take his vital signs. They'll clean him up, clamp the umbilical cord, and take his measurements. At one minute after birth and again at five minutes after birth, they'll measure his Apgar scores. Your doctor will rate your baby on his color (healthy and pink or bluish), pulse, breathing, whether he cries or reacts to stimulation, and his muscle tone (does he kick/move his limbs, or does he just lie there). A healthy baby will have an Apgar score of seven or higher. However, even if your baby's first score is lower at first, it will probably rise for the five-minute score.

And the Moment You've All Been Waiting For . . .

You've waited nine months to see your baby. This is the moment you've so ~~impatiently~~ anxiously awaited. When the doctor places your baby, fresh from the birth canal, on your chest, you may be a little shocked at what you see. Now don't get me wrong, you'll undoubtedly think your little one is the most beautiful baby you've ever seen in your life; but still, it can be a little disconcerting when, at first glance, you realize your baby doesn't look like the ones in those Gerber ads.

If you're handed your baby before a nurse has cleaned her up, you'll probably notice a white coating that looks kind of like diaper cream covering your baby. This protected her sensitive skin while she soaked in amniotic fluid for nine months. The earlier your baby is born, the more of this white coating she'll have. Don't worry, the nurse will clean it off soon. If your baby has a lot of it, you may still find traces in her skin folds for days to come. It's okay, though; it'll give you something to do (cleaning white goop out of ears and armpits) while you're nursing your baby in the days to come.

You may also be somewhat surprised to see that your baby's head is a little pointed. Being squeezed through the birth canal usually molds Baby's head into a cone shape. Don't worry, your baby is not destined to look like the *Saturday Night Live* Coneheads for life. This slight pointiness will go away within a couple weeks. If your baby was born via cesarean section, he won't have the pointy head because he wasn't squeezed through the birth canal. Unless you ended up having an emergency C-section after hours of labor and pushing.

> It can be a little disconcerting when, at first glance, you realize your baby doesn't look like the ones in those Gerber ads.

One of the first things you'll probably notice about your baby's appearance is the color and amount of hair she has. Because of the old wives' tale about heartburn, which I mentioned in Chapter 5, I thought that Savannah was going to be a really hairy baby, and she actually was. She not only had a full head of hair, but she had fine hair on her shoulders and back and even on her ears. In fact, we called her "wolf girl" for a while because of the hair on her ears. (I'm sure she'll appreciate the fact that I just wrote that little tidbit in here.)

Whether your baby has a head full of hair or he's nearly bald, he'll lose all that soft newborn hair in the following weeks. You'll probably be able to notice little strands of hair on your baby's sheets. Most babies will develop a very thin spot on the back of their head as they lose hair there. Don't worry, though; he won't have to do the "comb-over" or join the Hair Club for Men because new hair will grow in soon enough.

Another thing I found odd looking in my newborns was their fingernails. Their fingernails are very soft, and they sort of connect to the skin on their fingers, which makes trimming them for the first time very difficult. You have to do it very carefully to prevent cutting your baby's fingers. Newborns' fingers and toes oftentimes have dry, peeling skin, too. Think how your hands would look if they'd been soaking in a tub full of warm water for nine months. It's normal.

Many newborns are born with pink spots on either their eyelids or the back of their neck. Pink spots on their eyelids are called angel kisses; if they're on the back of the neck, they're called stork bites. These fade away over time.

When the nurse is done taking Baby's measurements,

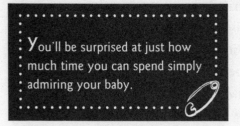

You'll be surprised at just how much time you can spend simply admiring your baby.

cleaning her up, and putting her hospital band on her, she'll swaddle her in a receiving blanket and hand her to you. Then you can really gaze at your little baby and marvel at how beautiful she is. You'll be surprised at just how much time you can spend simply admiring your baby. It's just so amazing to think that you made her, that she grew inside you, and more important, *that she came out of you*! I remember just looking in amazement at my baby, wondering how on earth she fit inside me. This whole other person was inside me! This whole other person came out of me! Seriously, it will astound you when you hold your little baby on your chest and try to imagine her fitting inside you. Sheesh, it's no wonder you were so uncomfortable!

It's a Gusher!

This is another thing that came as a big shock to me after I gave birth to my first son. I knew there would be some bleeding after giving birth, but I wasn't prepared for the amount of blood. The first time you stand up after giving birth, don't be shocked to see five gallons of blood drip down your legs. Okay, well maybe it isn't quite five gallons, but it really can be a shock to see the volume of blood that comes out. They call it lochia, and technically it isn't just blood, but a combination of blood, mucus, and tissue from your uterus. For the next few days, every time you get up, expect to have a gush of blood. This is normal and will taper off after a few days to a light pink discharge that will completely disappear after a couple weeks.

Another thing you should be told is what your nurses will do to you soon after you give birth. No one told me about this when I was pregnant with my first child. I'm here to give you a heads-up. Your nurses will massage your abdomen. And by "massage," I mean, they will press down on your belly really, really hard. This makes your uterus contract and shrink back down, pinching off blood vessels and helping to stop the bleeding. I won't lie to you; as your nurse does this, it will hurt. A lot! As she pushes down on your tummy, you'll feel blood rush out, and you'll probably want to pass out from the pain of her pressure on your abdomen.

Because your nurse ~~is basically cruel~~ wants to make sure you don't have any postpartum hemorrhaging, she'll come back and do this several times the first day after delivery. With my last two babies, I tried hiding out in the bathroom when it was time for my nurse to come in and torture me, but it didn't work. Every time I stuck my head out the door to see if the coast was clear she'd grab me and "massage" my uterus.

Breastfeeding

When I asked my friends what they remembered about breastfeeding, they all said the same thing: Make sure you tell everyone the truth! Tell them how hard it is when you first start! No one warned me about this!

Okay, so I'm going to tell you the truth. Although everyone makes it seem like breastfeeding is the most natural, automatic thing you can do, it does not come easily to everyone. Many of us end up wishing we'd taken a college course on breastfeeding before having our babies. Yes, it's a natural act, but it takes some practice to do it comfortably and confidently. Too many of my friends dissolved into tears and felt like a failure when breastfeeding didn't go smoothly the first time they tried it. I'm here to say, do *not* feel like a failure if you and Baby don't catch on immediately. You are not alone! And just because you may start off rocky, don't think that it won't get any better. Although many women get off to a tentative start with breastfeeding, most women go on to have an awesome, fulfilling time in the long run.

Now, I don't want you to read this and think that breastfeeding is hard and not worth the effort. Breastfeeding isn't hard—not by a long shot. It just takes a little practice to get it down. So, although you may have trouble the first few times, by the time your baby is a couple weeks old, you'll be a pro! You'll be able to walk around the house breastfeeding Baby with one arm, writing thank-you notes with the other one, while talking on the phone and making a delicious tapenade to serve your visitors. It's true.

If breastfeeding doesn't come automatically the first time or two, don't worry. Instead, enlist the help of the nurses or lactation consultants. Don't worry that you'll be too self-conscious to let a stranger help you get your baby to latch on. After giving birth, modesty is pretty much a thing of the past. Breastfeeding, when done properly, shouldn't cause any pain. If you're experiencing pain and frustration, believe me, you'll welcome the help. The nursing staff is trained to help you with breastfeeding questions and problems, and most hospitals have lactation consultants on hand who will see you at least once during your hospital stay (and probably more often if you're having trouble and request help).

Reading books on breastfeeding or taking a class about it beforehand can help you to understand the whole process, but won't necessarily eliminate any possible problems. With breastfeeding, you pretty much just have to get in there and give it a try. You learn from doing. Still, it never hurts to be prepared, and if your hospital offers such a class, you might want to take advantage of it.

You'll probably want to have a good breast pump also. While I was breastfeeding my first baby, I took a class once a week. My parents watched my baby while I attended class. I pumped milk so my parents could give him a bottle while I was at class. Of course, he was stubborn and refused the bottle week after week and instead would just scream until I got home. Many nights, my parents ended up buckling him in their car and driving around the block numerous times until he fell asleep. Sorry, I digress.

If you go back to work after having your baby and you want to continue to breastfeed him, you'll definitely need a very good pump. Even if you're a stay-at-home mom of other kids and don't plan on being separated from your new baby, it's nice to have a pump on hand, just in case. If you want to go on a date with your hubby or shopping with a girlfriend and you're going to miss a feeding, you'll want to have a bottle on hand for the caregiver to feed your baby. You can use formula, if you like, or breast milk that's been pumped.

I have a friend, Debra, who was never able to breastfeed her baby, but she still really wanted him to have breast milk as opposed to formula. The answer for her was to pump milk and feed him bottles. This worked well for her because her husband was able to give their baby bottles, too. I have another friend, Nancy, who insists that it's perfectly acceptable to throw the pump at your husband if he mooos at you while you're pumping. I agree with her.

Know What Hurts Worse Than Labor?

Afterpains! Afterpains is what they call it when your uterus contracts and shrinks back down after giving birth. I don't call them afterpains. I call them "PAIN THAT IS WORSE THAN LABOR!" Afterpains usually aren't too bad in first-time moms, but the pain tends to worsen the more kids you have. Although I'd made it through labor without any pain medication, I found myself needing some to deal with the afterpains with my fifth and sixth babies.

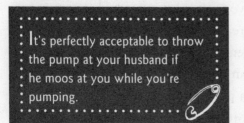

It's perfectly acceptable to throw the pump at your husband if he moos at you while you're pumping.

When you breastfeed, oxytocin is released, which causes your uterus to contract, so afterpains are much more painful while breastfeeding. When I breastfed my last three or four kids, I literally doubled over in pain for the first week or so after giving birth. Yes, it really hurts, but it's a good thing because it helps shrink your uterus back down to where it belongs. And, the good news is, these afterpains won't last until you wean your baby. They'll diminish in intensity and finally, in a couple weeks, subside.

Recovering from an Episiotomy

I didn't have an episiotomy with my fourth baby, mainly because my doctor wasn't there before I pushed her out. I didn't have episiotomies with my last two babies either, because I threatened bodily harm to the doctor if he dared to come near me with a pair of scissors. The difference in recovery between the times I had an episiotomy and the times I didn't—night and day.

After suffering such trauma down there (like pushing a baby with a thirteen-inch head circumference out of a hole that is ordinarily NOT thirteen inches wide, having your delicate tissue cut with a pair of scissors and then sewed back up with a needle and thread), you'll find it difficult to get around. Walking slowly and like a penguin might help a bit. Actually, it won't really help the pain at all, but you won't be able to walk any other way for a few days. What does help ease the pain are the tools your nurse will give you—a squirt bottle, witch hazel pads, and Epifoam. If someone had told me that I would come to love a little plastic squirt bottle almost as much as my baby, I would've thought they were nuts. But trust me on this one, you will fall in love with your bottle. There is nothing quite so soothing on tender tissue than a stream of warm water. You'll be using this bottle every time you go to the bathroom for a long time.

In fact, for the first day or two after giving birth, using your squirt bottle *while* going to the bathroom will help immeasurably. Spraying a constant stream of warm water over the whole area can really help. See, this is the stuff no one tells you before you have a baby. After you give birth, you'll be scared to use the bathroom. You'll be sore and you'll be afraid of pulling stitches, if you have any, and you'll be afraid that urinating will cause more pain. With my first three babies, a nurse insisted on keeping me company in the bathroom while I urinated for the first time. For ~~normal people~~ many of us, it's difficult to pee in front of an audience.

It's often hard to urinate soon after giving birth because your bladder has been squished during delivery or because you're sore from your episiotomy, or because you're just kind of numb down there and don't really feel like going. If you think peeing is scary, just wait until you have to have a bowel movement (and you will have to eventually because most hospitals won't let you leave until you assure them that you can). I know, I know. First, I stressed that you might have a bowel movement during delivery, and then I stress that you can't have a bowel movement after delivery. Ugh. Eat plenty of fiber and drink a lot of liquids—which won't be hard to

> Walking slowly and like a penguin might help.

do if you're nursing, because you'll probably find yourself exceedingly thirsty all the time. And relax, you're not going to split your stitches.

I have some friends who insisted they needed a little doughnut pillow to sit on after they had their babies. Yes, the pain from an episiotomy or tear can really be that bad. On the bright side, like everything else, it won't last forever. Just continue to use that soothing Epifoam or line your pad with a couple witch hazel pads and take it easy for a couple weeks. You're going to be tired from labor and delivery and waking throughout the night to feed your new baby anyway, so rest is what you're going to want and need for the next couple weeks.

Tiredness

Remember back when you were first pregnant? Of course, you don't. It's all part of the pregnancy amnesia. But try to think back a few months. Remember that bone-tired feeling you had in the first trimester? Remember thinking that you'd never been so tired in all your life? Well, guess what? You'll probably feel even more tired now. After giving birth, most women are pretty darn exhausted, especially if they went through several hours of hard labor and/or pushing. Think about what your body has done. It's no wonder you're exhausted. Giving birth takes a lot out of you.

You go through labor and delivery with no food, which doesn't help in the tiredness department. Depending on when you went into labor, you may have missed out on a

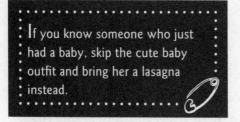

If you know someone who just had a baby, skip the cute baby outfit and bring her a lasagna instead.

couple nights' sleep by the time you give birth. Your body has surely worked harder than that of any triathlete. And now it's working hard to make milk so you can feed your baby.

Expect to be tired ~~forever~~ several weeks. Rest when you can. Take a nap when Baby naps. Hire someone to come clean your house for you or take your mother up on her offer to clean. But be forewarned: when your mother offers to come over and clean, she really means "sit there and hold the baby all day leaving you free to clean." Gratefully accept any offered meals. In fact, that was my very favorite gift of all time when I had my babies. It wasn't that I didn't like flowers or baby clothes or diapers or anything, but the thing I most appreciated were the meals my family and friends brought to me when I got home from the hospital. If you know someone who just had a baby, skip the cute baby outfit and bring her a lasagna instead. She'll love you forever for it!

Sweating

Remember back when you were pregnant? Remember how swollen your ankles were? Remember all the fluids you were retaining? Well, now that Baby's here, it's time for those fluids to come out. This is why, when you're lying in your hospital bed, you will find yourself sweating so much, you stick to the plastic mattress. My friends and I all experienced night sweats after giving birth. We'd wake up in the middle of the night, hot and drenched in sweat. Sometimes it was to the point we needed to get up and take a shower. Some nights, I'd drape a towel over my bed before lying down for the night.

Your sweating will probably be the worst during the week after you give birth, gradually tapering off. I think it lasted off and on for a good month after I gave birth to my kiddos. Just make sure you drink plenty of fluids during the day to replace those you've sweat out during the night.

Hair Loss

Gone are the luxurious locks from your pregnant days. You just went through nine months without a strand of hair falling out. Your hair was bright and shiny, thick and healthy. Say good-bye to that. Your hair will now make up for lost time and will fall out by the handful. Don't be too concerned if you find hair in your brush, on the bathroom counters, in your sink, and on the floor. If you see a wad of hair the size of a small mammal in the shower drain, it's normal. It happens. Eventually, it'll slow down and get back to normal. Well, to prepregnancy normal anyway.

Losing Weight

I physically cringe to write this part. I'm not sure how much advice I can give you on losing pregnancy weight when I still haven't lost my pregnancy weight from my first child who is now fifteen years old. Of course, it didn't help that I had five more babies after him, all less than three years apart. Still, I'm pretty sure I didn't carry any of them in my butt and that seems to be where all my weight has settled. So I really don't have an excuse.

When my first son was one month old, I took him to the mall to get professional pictures taken. I did that back when I had only one child. I made sure I had his pictures taken every couple months. I recorded his milestones in his baby book. My second baby has a few firsts recorded in her baby book. By the time the fourth was born, I neglected to record a single thing in her book. And don't ask me about my sixth. I never even *got* a baby book for her!

Anyway, I held my month-old infant in my arms as I awaited our turn in front of the camera. The reception-ist took a look at my son and commented, "Awww, he's so cute!"

I smiled. *Of course he's cute.* New parents think their baby is the cutest baby ever to be born and believe everyone should agree.

She glanced down at my still sizable postpartum abdomen and excitedly asked, "Oh, when are you due?"

Okay yes, this girl was clearly not too bright to assume I was several months pregnant when I was holding my new-born infant. But still, this is *not* the kind of thing a new mom wants to hear. Ever.

I squelched the urge to yell, "I am NOT pregnant! Are you stupid? I'm holding my ONE-month-old baby, for crying out loud!" Instead, those good ole hormones took over and I started crying. It's depressing enough that you can't fit into your jeans after you give birth, but for someone to think

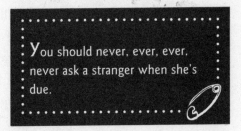

You should never, ever, ever, never ask a stranger when she's due.

you're still pregnant a month after you gave birth is just plain devastating. This is why you should never, ever, ever, never ask a stranger when she's due. I don't care if that stranger is at the baby store registering for cribs, do not ask her when she's due. She might just be carrying around a few extra Thanksgiving pounds while helping her sister register for baby items. Even if the stranger in question is carrying a baby names book and looks like she's going to give birth any minute, you do not ask her when she's due. Period. Ever.

Ready for Another One?

I remember thinking, while I was in labor with my first baby, that I would never, ever have any more kids. Although I had wanted two children when I first got married, I decided there was no way I could go through pregnancy and delivery again. No way. No sir. But somehow, all those thoughts disappeared the first moment I held my baby and looked at his perfect little face. Clearly, I forgot all about my not wanting to ever go through labor and delivery again because I have six kids now. Some days I think I'd like six more. Of course, there are other days, I think I'd like six less. . . .

The good news is that you will forget most of the unpleasant and painful memories of pregnancy. Even if you have an incredible memory and can recall every line from the time you played a carrot in the kindergarten play, "Veggies Are Our Friends," you will forget how your feet swelled up in pregnancy. You'll forget how you burst out crying on the train in front of three dozen people because a woman in front of you was holding a baby. You'll forget about the heartburn, the fatigue, and most important, the pain of childbirth. This "pregnancy amnesia" is a good kind of forgetfulness. Without this, no one in their right mind would have more than one child. And really, who wants to pack away all those cute baby clothes? It's much easier to just have another baby to pass them on to than to haul them up to the attic. Besides, this is the perfect excuse to keep those last ten pregnancy pounds. "Why should I bother losing it now when I'm just going to get pregnant again?"

A grand adventure is about to begin.
—Winnie-the-Pooh

*There is only one pretty child in the world
and every mother has it.*
—Chinese proverb

CHAPTER 15

~~THE END~~ IT'S JUST THE BEGINNING

Congratulations on joining the ranks of other mothers. There's just something about childbirth that brings women together. No matter what your individual circumstances are, there's something universal about the whole experience.

And mothers like nothing more than sharing their childbirth stories with other women. Just like when you first announced your pregnancy, and mothers came out of the woodwork to share their stories with you, it's now your turn to share your stories with others. And you won't just share the story of your baby's delivery. Oh no, you'll share details about your heartburn and morning sickness. You'll tell other women the intimate details of your episiotomy, how your breasts are sore, and all about your constipation. And you know what? It won't even seem weird to you or to the other moms with whom you share your tales. It's a bond you'll share.

We're an elite group of underpaid, underappreciated, hardworking women. You've gone through pregnancy, labor, and delivery, but your job is just beginning. Your life will never be the same. You will always be someone's mother. It doesn't matter how old that child gets, you will still be his mom. Even when that child grows up, leaves the house, and has children of his own, you'll still be his mom. The responsibility is overwhelming. You have your work cut out for you. But the rewards are immeasurable. You have been blessed with the gift of a miracle. Enjoy it!

Whether this is your only baby or you go on to have more in the future, enjoy this job they call motherhood. It's the best one you'll ever have!

ACKNOWLEDGMENTS

This book wouldn't have come about without the help and encouragement of several people:

God, who has blessed me in so very many ways;

my children, who gave me heartburn, nausea, varicose veins, and stretch marks. I wouldn't trade any of it for all the gold in the world (I might consider trading it for a nap, however);

my family, who supported me and encouraged me to write;

my friends, especially my girlfriends, who have shared their pregnancy and delivery stories with me;

my awesome agent, Janet Kobobel Grant, who I'm convinced is some sort of miracle worker;

my incredible editor Philis Boultinghouse, who finished fixing my mess of a manuscript, and my equally wonderful editor Beth Adams, who started fixing it. Without them, you'd be reading a book that talked about poop on every other page and included the phrase "trust me" at least 50,000 times;

my blog readers, who continue to read the nonsense I blog about and who take the time to comment and share their own stories with me;

and especially Jonathan Merkh, Jennifer Willingham, and my friends at Howard, who have invested themselves in this book and me, and the good folks at *Guideposts*.

ABOUT THE AUTHOR

Dawn Meehan lives with her six children on the outskirts of Chicago, where she practices her juggling skills daily. On any given evening, Dawn can be found taking one child to cheerleading practice, dropping off another at church, making dinner, going to the grocery store, paying the bills, kissing a boo-boo, reading a bedtime story, cleaning up muddy footprints, folding laundry, taking a child to the ER, and explaining to her kids why they can't have an indoor Slip 'n Slide or a pet squirrel.

After Dawn auctioned a pack of Pokémon cards on eBay, she attracted the attention of nearly a hundred thousand readers in one day. Her blog, BecauseISaidSo.com, skyrocketed to become one of the most popular mommy blogs on the net. In 2008 her blog was voted the Best Parenting Blog by the Blogger's Choice Awards. It has been nominated for the Best Humor Blog, the Hottest Mommy Blogger, the Best Parenting Blog, and the Best Blog of All Time for the past three years. In 2009 her blog was nominated for the Funniest Blog by BlogLuxe, and Dawn was named one of the top thirty-five Mommy Bloggers by Babble. Her kids think the blog is just okay.

Journaling My Own Pregnancy Experience

Journaling My Own Pregnancy Experience

Journaling My Own Pregnancy Experience

Journaling My Own Pregnancy Experience
· ·

Journaling My Own Pregnancy Experience

Journaling My Own Pregnancy Experience

Journaling My Own Pregnancy Experience

Journaling My Own Pregnancy Experience